A DIALOGUE ON SCIENCE,
PSYCHOLOGY AND GOD

A DIALOGUE ON SCIENCE, PSYCHOLOGY AND GOD

Walter R. Thompson

PHILOSOPHICAL LIBRARY
New York

INTRODUCTION

The investigation in this book follows its own course. Its dialogue form has not been fixed by philosophical tradition and certainly such form possesses no literary expediency. The subject
matter, since it attempts the synthesis of ideas from quite disparate
disciplines, lends itself to an Hegelian dialectic. For this reason I
trust that the inherent difficulties of the dialogue form will not
prove too great an impediment to the reader.

The passages quoted were selected in the main from the popular
literature of science and psychology. The writer's investigative
techniques, insofar as philosophy is concerned, were developed
as a pupil of Bertrand Russell and Ludwig Wittgenstein. I am
grateful to Russell for referring me during the book's preparation
to the passages from St. Augustine. As he has pointed out these
are generally omitted by most editors as unimportant.*

The work professes no originality in epistemology, logic or science. It nevertheless contains, I think, two or three original
thoughts on the synthesis of ideas from these subjects with theology. One cannot perhaps attempt a synthesis of ideas from the
wide field of philosophy, the physical and biological sciences, psychology and theology without inviting criticism from specialists in
each of the fields. It seems to me, however, that the effort to per-
form such a unification should be of sufficient interest, even to specialists, to outweigh criticism of the depth of treatment, unless indeed some important idea has been overlooked. One must make a
nice distinction as to the level of competence in the specialized fields
at which one is able to (or should) attempt a synthesis. I cannot
say that the line I have drawn is a good one. Indeed, the treatment
may well be superficial, since the ideal level would be complete

* Letter to the author, June, 1965.

1

competence in all fields. I have drawn the line where I think the educated layman would draw it, that is, as a stranger to the specialist fields. I have done this because it is my conviction that a rationale of all knowledge is within the reach of all men.

W.R.T.
Coquitlam, B.C.
Canada

Eirat

Where shall we begin? Shall we go along the planes of space and down the winds of time, watching electrons dance in a never ending line?

Dymon

Nothing so poetic—you've undoubtedly thought about death. Let's start with that. What does death mean to you?

Eirat

Yes, I've thought about it—in the same way that a child thinks about taking medicine. I've tried to see the necessity for it and consequently have learned that I wouldn't even be here if it weren't for "death". As you know, micro-organisms from which we have evolved reproduced asexually. Asexual cells may be destroyed but they don't die. They keep reproducing indefinitely with the same monotonous characteristics. Evolution, if there is to be any in asexual cells, must be through the occasional mutant cell. But look what happens when sexual reproduction and death are developed to assist in the evolutive process. Through the agency of death, organisms can evolve. Natural selection and adaptation can operate only if organisms die. Without death, there would be little to choose from the organic stock and, more important, no mechanism for exercising the choice. If we, in our present form, represent some three billion years of chemical and biological evolution, we do so only because death has been the means of selecting us from the organic stockpile. Sexual reproduction provided a continuous supply of clay and death was the sculptor's tool. Next to reproduction, death must surely rank as the greatest invention of nature.

Dymon

Aptly put! You don't believe in a life or a place hereafter, I take it.

Eirat

Certainly not in any conventional sense. If there were such a place, it would obviously be inhabited not only by man, the evolutive finished product, but by all the adaptive and selective rejects as well. And why should it not also be inhabited by trilobites, dodo birds, dinosaurs and Neanderthal men. If we restrict the hereafter to humans as we know them, we would be insufferable snobs; if we allow in all the blind ends and rejects of evolution, it would be an over-populated garbage heap.

3

Dymon

Let's examine the concept in more detail. Frankly, you disappoint me if this is all you can say of it.

Eirat

What more would you like to know? In the light of our present knowledge the "hereafter" is absurd. It was enunciated in a different time and age to serve the psychological need of persons for whom life was very different. The idea is not peculiar to Christendom, it forms part of many religions. But what does it mean? First of all, a "life hereafter" presupposes that "life" goes on after it has ceased to be "life". That is, I take it, it continues to exist in some form other than life as we know it. What then, is "life" as we know it?

Dymon

You've put the question, let's see you answer it.

Eirat

Well, if I can't answer the question, I think I can, nevertheless, circumscribe it. I take it you will agree that what we mean by "life" including man, has evolved through other species from some organism of submicroscopic size. If this be the case, we must go further. Since A. I. Oparin's book "Origin of Life", there has been no sharp differentiation in the minds of microbiologists between living and non-living matter, and if the organic world developed from the inorganic, it makes little sense to ask what life is. It is simply organic matter which has been organized from inorganic salts and colloidal compounds by the action of energy dating from the time the earth first began to cool.

Dymon

How so? Would you be good enough to sketch Oparin's case for me?

Eirat

I'll do my best. The problem for Oparin was how living organisms arose spontaneously from inorganic substances. If we grant the existence of ocean water, and some of the salts found therein; if we also imagine that in the fargone era of pre-history, there was continual energy bombardment of the ocean from electrical disturbances and radiation, we can, by present experimental processes, see that there would of necessity have been produced simple compounds such as amino acids.

4

Though the preponderant tendency would be toward dissolution of such compounds into their constituent elements, nevertheless, through a tendency to aggregate and organize, their equilibrium became oriented towards more complex structural aggregates—almost as though a biological equivalent of gravity were functioning.

Oparin suggested that at this level the aggregates competed with one another for additional molecules and further that considerations of optimal size began to operate. A colloidal particle might, due to its increased size, become unstable and break down into its constituent parts, growing and dividing again. Such a particle to live, that is to say, to be the situs of an influx and outflow of matter and energy, must derive food from its surrounding. This, it is suggested, may have been accomplished by fermentation. After further stretches of time, the process of photosynthesis was developed. This enabled the complex colloidal aggregate to make its own organic molecules for food. With photosynthesis came oxygen as a by-product, and with oxygen organisms developed the respiratory process. It seems obvious that if this be the general evolutive process, then a "life hereafter" is a contradiction of terms. We are apparently on this planet because physical, chemical and biological processes have combined to produce us. We humans and other species, in our main physiological development, have apparently come inexorably off nature's assembly line. And if, as we said earlier, death played a critical role in the latter part of this story of life, then what meaning can be attributed to a life after death? Incidentally, while we are on the question of "origin of life", I'd like you to note what Oparin's translator Sergius Morgulius has to say on the concepts "origin" and "life".

" 'Origin', especially to those brought up in the biblical tradition, implies, a finite and sharply delineated event of creation, not a process extending over infinite time. Modern paleontologists tell us that evolution of living things, which has blossomed out with a profusion of plant and animal species of almost endless variety, has occupied a period of something like a billion years. The Earth has retained an unmistakable record of this for nearly half a billion years. It will aid the reader to orient himself with regard to the evolution of species to be reminded that in this inconceivably long span of half a billion years, registered in the Earth's crust by some historical remains, the footmarks left by man and his close predecessors encompass barely one million years, perhaps two-tenths of one percent.* But the origination of life, which is the subject matter of Oparin's book, precedes by about another billion years the story of the 'Origin of Species' in which Darwin picks up the thread, and of this earlier period there is no existing record. While Darwin's is a well documented story and his ideas, though highly controversial, can be bolstered with substantial factual material, Oparin's story embracing probably another billion years, lacks the support of ascertainable facts. By its very nature, a theory of how life had come into being must be highly speculative. Lacking a solid factual basis, the soundness or acceptability of such a theory can only be judged by whether or not, or to what extent, it conforms to the criterion of reasonable consistency with established knowledge in various fields of scientific inquiry. The origin of life was not an occurrence ascribable to some definite place and time; it was a gradual process operating upon the Earth over an inconceivably long span of time, a process of unfolding which consumed perhaps more millions of years than was required for the evolution of all the species of living things. It is one of Oparin's great contributions to the theory of the origin of life that he postulated a long chemical evolution as a necessary preamble to the emergence of Life. One might think of the evolutionary process passing through three distinct chemical phases, from inorganic chemistry to organic chemistry and from organic chemistry to biological chemistry. And it is true that if the organic chemist is familiar with wonders undreamed of by the inorganic chemist, the wonders witnessed by the biochemist in his daily tasks stagger the imagination and sharpen the envy of the organic chemist. These transitions in the history of our Earth were not isolated events but a continuous flux requiring eons for their realization. In interpreting the significance of the word 'origin' one must free oneself of the cultural tradition and conceive it as something entirely outside the ordinary human framework of time.

The second misconception stems from associations clustering about the word 'Life'. To most people Life connotes something that crawls, creeps or at least wiggles if not by means of well articulated appendages at any rate by temporary protoplasmic protrusions, or cilia, or delicate flagella. Life need not perhaps be visualized in the form of a stalking elephant but to the human it may seem inconceivable except

* Morgulius was of course writing before the discovery by Louis S. B. Leakey of Homo Habilis (1.75 million years) and by Bryan Patterson of Kanapoi Hominid (2.5 million years).

6

as some unicellular organism of microscopic dimensions. But even the most primitive unicellular organism has a complexity of structure and function that staggers the mind and is removed from the beginnings of Life by a genealogy extending for millions upon millions of years. Possibly, as Oparin so convincingly tells us, it all began some two billion years ago as a venture in colloidal systems of microscopic size separating from the 'hot thin soup', to use Haldane's happy description of the primordial ocean.

The biologist, unlike the layman, knows no lines of demarcation separating plant life from animal life, nor for that matter living from non-living material, because such differentiations are purely conceptual and do not correspond to reality."

Dymon

So be it—you recognize the logical absurdity of individual immortality. Is that the end of it? Is there no room in your scheme of things for the religious impulse?

Eirat

What do you mean by religious impulse?

Dymon

Very well, since you apparently wish to philosophize, we'll leave that topic for a moment while I try to determine if you have *experienced* a religious impulse as distinct from whether or not you can articulate it.

I have a quotation for you. It is from the opening of Genesis:

"In the beginning God created the heavens and the earth."

What sense, if any, do you attribute to that statement? Was its Hebrew author [1] suggesting that some superior being by a conscious act created space and matter? [2]

Eirat

Possibly something of the like. But before we criticize him, let's try to understand the author. Imagine him sitting some six thousand years ago on a mountain, like Moses, and looking about him

[1] St. Augustine attributes this statement to Moses, rather than as is now accepted, to an unknown predecessor of Moses.
[2] Augustine dealt with several interpretations of these words. I have selected one in which Augustine criticized himself on other grounds. Book 12, para. 29, *Confessions*.

7

with wonder.[3] What more natural than that he should, speculating without the aid of a highly sophisticated physics, biology and paleontology and a highly developed mathematical culture, postulate the simple act of an outside agency as a creator? It apparently solved all the problems. Let us now look at his statement on its merits. If God created the heaven and the earth, then as St. Augustine asks (and answers) [4], what was God doing before he did this? And even more puzzling, "Who created God?"

Dymon

Since you ask that the statement be looked at on its merits, I suggest that it's not to be shrugged off by saying "Who created God?" You'll have to do better than that.

Eirat

Yes, and I think I can. Any theory of the universe known to cosmology or religion is predicated upon a "beginning". But what is a "beginning"? The concept presupposes an observer. An observer is peculiar to "life" as we have discussed it. A beginning makes no sense in the absence of someone to observe it. Some people will quarrel with this, of course; they will say, "I can perfectly well imagine an unpopulated world in which it makes sense to speculate upon its beginning." I submit, however, that such people are themselves the "observer" in such a world. Who was the observer in the case the Hebrew speaks of? He says in effect that God created space and matter. Or let us pretend that he said that in order to cloak his statement with scientific respectability. He therefore postulated a theory of the creation of space and matter. But what of time? Does he say that God created time also? No! Time is the suppressed premise in his statement. He says that "In the *beginning* God created, etc." So time was already there? It was there, but it had just begun? Is that it? Well, what does physics say? It equates mass with energy. So if we use terminology of this century, we can say that "the earth" to the Hebrew meant mass-energy while "the heavens" meant space. Therefore,

---

[3] The earliest known hieroglyphics appear to be dated around 3500 B.C. The cuneiform code of King Khammurabi appears to be dated around 2200 B.C.
[4] Augustine answers by saying, "But if before heaven and earth there was no time, why is it demanded what thou then didst? For there was nothing when there was no time." Book 12, para. 13, *Confessions*.

he was saying, "In the *beginning* God created space and mass-energy." He thus makes the same mistake that everyone following him made until Einstein appeared. They thought of time as a separate dimension from space. That's what the Hebrew did. He was thinking of three dimensions of space operating in a fourth dimension, time. He could also be accused of thinking of "time" as existing prior to the creation of space and mass-energy.[5]

Dymon

I accept your analysis thus far, but you've offered no substitute for this cosmology. If you intend, for example, to discuss evolution—whether it be the evolution of species, the evolution of organic matter from the inorganic, or the birth and death of stars and galaxies, you've still got to come to grips with "time", for "time" is the yardstick you use. You must be careful not to make the same mistake the Hebrew did. It makes no sense for you to suggest on the one hand that "time" is a concomitant of space in a four dimensional continuum and yet go on using "time" in all your other branches of science—in the Newtonian sense of three dimensions of space operating in one of time.

Eirat

I agree with you. And before we go much farther we should therefore look more closely at "time" as a physical concept. People are often puzzled about certain of the statements made by physicists about "time". Einstein, probably, started their difficulties with statements like this:

"The experiences of an individual appear to us arranged in a series of events; in this series the single events which we remember appear to be ordered according to the criterion of 'earlier' or 'later'. There exists therefore, for the individual an I—Time, or subjective time. This in itself is not measurable. I can, indeed, associate numbers with events, in such a way that a greater number is associated with a later event than the earlier one. This association I can define by means of a clock by comparing the order of events furnished by the clock with the order of the given series of events."

The implication to some is that there is something deficient about subjective time, that it is really a very inferior sort of time—different from the objective time of the physicist. From such state-

[5] Augustine also took issue with this interpretation. He said, "Yet was it (heaven and earth) not made just in time; because the forms of things give rise to time." Book 12, para. 29, *Confessions*.

ments, the argument proceeds that since an hour according to a clock is actually a measurement of space, namely 15 degrees of arc in the rotation of the earth, that there is indeed no such thing as a fixed interval of time independent of the system to which it is referred. Accordingly, it is stated that the scientist, whose task it is to describe physical events in objective terms, must rely upon the four dimensional geometry of Minkowski rather than upon egocentric words like "this" or "now". So far, so good. There is no quarrel with a physicist using a four dimensional geometry. It is more accurate and more useful for physical purposes than Cartesian three dimensional geometry. Certainly it is more useful than words like "this" or "now" for describing physical phenomena. But some do not stop at this point. They say, "We'll never really be able to understand the world we live in because it is four dimensional and the most that any of us can envisage is three. No one can build a model of a curved four dimensional space-time continuum. All they can do is make an approximate projection of it. For example, a photograph of a man is a projection in two dimensions of a person who lives in three space dimensions. In like manner, we can project four dimensions in our three of space. But no one can ever really *see* the four dimensions."

Dymon

Yes, I've read a good deal of that sort of thing. Is it then not accurate?

Eirat

It is misleading in two distinct ways. Firstly, what would it be like to *see* something in four dimensions? I expect that to do so we'd have to have our viewer viewing from a further dimension, namely, the fifth—just as a viewer situate now in the fourth dimension, namely, in time, observes therein the duration of events in the three dimensions of space. The event in the three dimensions of space, is observed with respect to its duration from the fourth.

The "I" of the observer is intelligible only in terms of time. If you doubt this, consider for a moment an observer in only two dimensions of space, that is, in a flat world. So long as there were an additional time dimension in which the "I" of that observer could observe the duration of events in his two spatial dimensions, such a world would be intelligible. So for us to see our world, including its time dimension as a model we would have to get *outside* the four dimensions which comprise it and observe it from an additional dimension. This, of course, is absurd. It appears therefore that our inability to envisage four dimensions is in no way a shortcoming of our minds. If we could envisage all four dimensions, there would have to be more than four. Consequently, although the physicist is correct in saying that we must treat the time axis in our four dimensional geometry in much the same way that we do the other three of space if we want accurate solutions to our physical problems, he is incorrect if he implies that it is a limitation of our minds that we are unable accurately to envisage this four dimensional world. It is not a limitation of our minds, it is the structure of the universe.

Dymon

I see what you mean. The physicist, by describing the phenomena in a four dimensional geometry, is able to discount the observer and the time dimension in which he is situate. Thus he can make his predictions just as he would if situate *outside* the world looking at it like a model.

Eirat

Precisely—while he cannot, even if it made sense to do so, remove himself bodily to an additional dimension in order to observe physical phenomena; he can do the next best thing, that is by adding a fourth axis for time to the three space axes of his geometry, he can accurately describe and predict physical phenomena without intrusion of "the observer" into his calculation. His statements are then accurate, as he says they are, independently of the frame of reference of the observer.

Dymon

But if space and time are, as Einstein says, the projections of an invariant four dimensional separation on corresponding axes of a four dimensional geometry, then this is true not only for physics but for all science. Perhaps you had best re-examine your concept of "beginning" when you use it in biology and cosmology.

Eirat

Well, I was about to re-examine "beginning". I was saying a moment ago that a "beginning" makes no sense in the absence of someone to observe it. What use do we normally make of "beginning"? We say, "The 'beginning' of the test mile is here." "This is the 'beginning' of the story." "That was the 'beginning' of the third movement." In all of these cases the "beginning" is the point in space or in time from where the measurement of the object or the

11

event commences. Einstein suggested that it is perhaps more accurate to speak of physical phenomena as being "point-events," a certain number of units of space-time removed from some other point-event. Whichever framework we use, we are in hot water immediately if we start asking where or when was the beginning of space or the beginning of time or indeed, of space-time, for we are asking for the logically impossible. We are asking a question about our frame of reference and expecting an answer in terms of that same frame of reference.

Dymon

I don't think you've clarified "beginning" or "time". You say only that if one asks questions *about* one's frame of reference one shouldn't expect an answer on or *in* that frame of reference. You should do more. By relating the character of the Hebrew's statement with cosmology, you may have created the impression that there is some language of higher order or a superior frame of reference in which it makes sense to talk of "the beginning of time". You should relate the question to its subjectivity like that of an ant condemned forever to live on the surface of a sphere. To the ant, the sphere's surface is his whole two dimensional world. Wander as he will, it has no beginning and no end in space.

Eirat

I think that mine is a better analogy than that of the ant confined to two dimensions. Let us expand it somewhat. Take a point in a three dimensional system and imagine that at this point is an observer. He then says, "I am now situate 'N' units in a positive direction along the 'X' axis. I am 'P' units in a positive direction along the 'Y' axis and 'Q' units positive along the 'Z' axis. These co-ordinates fix my position in terms of a geometric framework comprising the three dimensions of space. The datum for the intersection of the axes is any arbitrarily chosen point." Such person is of course using the Cartesian system implicit in the Hebrew's statement. Therefore, to complete the description, he must add a statement about time. He must say, "And I am at this point at 0200 hours."

Consider then this same person describing phenomena in space and time in terms of the corresponding axes of a *four*-dimensional geometry, as physics says he should. This person is wholly inside these four dimensions. There is no observer outside and these four dimensions comprise the whole universe. "Time" is simply one of the four co-ordinates necessary to fix his position in space-time, and in such geometry the time axis is not essentially different from the other three. This person then says, "In the beginning (of time) the sky was black." Does this statement make sense? If he had spoken of the beginning of a race, his statement would make sense, for the co-ordinates of that point-event could be given *within* his framework. Similarly, if he had spoken of the beginning of the test mile or the third movement, the co-ordinates of those point-events could be given in his framework. But this is not what he's done. He's spoken of the "beginning" of "time". And "time" is itself one of the axes of his framework. His statement, therefore, makes no sense. He's trying to say something *about* the framework in language which only has meaning with reference to phenomena *within* the framework.

Dymon

Yes, but you said that Einstein's disparagement of "subjective time" was misleading in *two* ways. You've illustrated only one. In what other way is it misleading?

Eirat

It is misleading in the second way because it dismisses "subjective time" as being immeasurable. Yet there are wide variations in "subjective time". Indeed from these variations, comparisons of biological time could be made. Suppose that our clocks were calibrated so that a year, instead of being astronomically based, was one seventieth of the life-span of any given observer. At the end of his life he would have had his own private calendar. You would then have a unit of biological time. Or take a human heart-beat and call it a second. Each would have his own "second". You could also have a human second as compared say to a sparrow second. Or take the life span of any free living cell and call it an hour. By some such system you might make comparisons of "subjective time". Let me quote, for example, what a biologist has said on the subject:

"A mouse and a man start alike as protoplasmic balls less than one-hundredth of an inch across. Both burn their brightest at the beginning and each expands with time. But mouse stuff is fully expanded within a few weeks and persists with ever lessening tension for two years at the most. Human stuff expands for about fifteen years, to reach much greater dimensions, and thereafer maintains its weakening vitality for another three-score years.

Giant tortoises, on the other hand, are something else, for the kind of time we are really concerned with is living time, not clock or calendar time. Tortoises and turtles and the vast majority of everything alive, everything in fact except mammals and birds, live at a pace dependent on the temperature of their surroundings and for most of their lives this is much lower than that of the two warm-blooded kinds. To make matters equal, the one hundred and fifty to two hundred calendar years of tortoise life should be reduced to a few decades. Even among the warmblooded, inequalities are obvious for time to a sloth is clearly different from time to a monkey, and a sparrow, for instance, lives literally at a hotter pace than a man.

Perhaps we have here the clue to the true meaning of time. We have clocks and calendars and almanacs, all of which measure the rate of spin of the earth about its axis or the circuit of the moon around the earth or the passage of the earth around the sun. Does it matter? Certainly we find it convenient to divide time of this sort into suitable packages and to be able to designate a particular moment for an assignment with a person or a train or for the meshing of procedures in an industry. Yet all of us feel that this is not a good reflection of time as we ourselves experience it. Childhood days are long, and youthful years are eternal compared with the racing sequence of later periods. Time must be measured by how fast things happen—the rapidity of events—and the rate of change. On this reckoning the greatest and fastest happenings of your whole existence took place during the first two or three weeks after you were conceived—everything since then has been comparatively routine and progressively staid. And slow. We should measure the time of our life not by how often a clock can tick while the earth turns completely round but by how much happens to us and in us as living organisms. How often your heart contracted and expanded, how many visual images came to your attention, how many times your interest shifted, how intensely you felt some physical pain and how quickly forgot it, how much joy did you feel and how often did that emotion come to you—how frequently were new cells born and how much memory went into storage. If you have ever watched a mouse with its whiskers vibrant and its nose atwitch, you will have sensed a quickness of living that is faster than your own. Mouse time is not man time, though both are living time. The meaning seems clear; when so-called time is empty, when nothing at all goes on, not even time has meaning. So it comes to this, that living time, which is what really matters to us, is measured by the amount of life rather than by the number of seconds or days or years; and life, being first and foremost activity and action, is to be estimated primarily as energy expended." [6]

[6] *You and the Universe,* N. J. Berrill, page 57.

Berrill says that when time is empty, when nothing at all goes on, not even time has meaning. This, of course, is just as true of astronomical time as it is of biological time. If planets, stars and galaxies were not in motion, astronomical time would also be meaningless. Time, whether biological or astronomical, as well as space, are not part of nature; they are part of the psychological apparatus with which we *observe* nature. They are peculiar to an observer. There is of course nothing new about this idea. Listen to St. Augustine writing in A.D. 397 on the question of "time".

"For what is time? Who can readily and briefly explain this? Who can even in thought comprehend it, so as to utter a word about it? But what in discourse do we mention more familiarly and knowingly than time? . . . What then is time? If no one asks me I know; if I wish to explain it to one that asketh, I know not; yet I say boldly that I know that, if nothing passed away, a time past were not; and if nothing were coming, a time to come were not; and if nothing were, time present were not."
("CONFESSIONS", Paragraph XIV)

"If an instant of time be conceived which cannot be divided into the smallest particles of moments, that alone is it, which may be called present. . . . the present hath no space."
(Paragraph XV)

"But we measure times as they are passing by perceiving them."
(Paragraph XVI)

"Present of things past, memory; present of things present, sight; present of things future, expectation."
(Paragraph XX)

"Yet what do we measure, if not time in some space? For we do not say single, double, and triple, and equal, or any other like way that we speak of time, except of spaces of time. In what space then do we measure time passing?"
(Paragraph XXI)

"I heard once from a learned man that the motions of the sun, moon, and stars constituted time, and I assented not. For why should not the motions of all bodies rather be times? Or, if the lights of heaven should cease and a potter's wheel run round, should there be no time by which we might measure those whirlings? . . . I ask does the motion alone make the day, or the stay in which that motion is completed, or both? For if the first be the day, then should we have a day, although the sun should finish that course in so small a space of time as one hour comes

to. If the second, then should that not make a day, if between one sunrise and another there were but so short a stay as one hour comes to. . . . If both, then neither could that be called a day, if the sun should run his whole round in the space of one hour; nor that, if, while the sun stood still, so much time should overpass as the sun usually makes his whole course in, from morning to morning. . . . Let no man then tell me that the motions of the heavenly bodies constitute times. . . . I perceive time then to be a certain extension."
(Paragraph XXIII)

"Seeing therefore the motion of a body is one thing, that by which we measure how long it is, another; who sees not which of the two is rather to be called time?"
(Paragraph XXIV)

"Do I then measure. . . . and not know what I measure? I measure the motion of a body in time; and the time itself I do not measure? . . . Do we by a shorter time measure a longer, as by the space of a cubit the space of a rood? Whence it seemed to me that time is nothing else than protraction; but of what, I know not; and I marvel if it be not of the mind itself?"
(Paragraph XXVI)

"For the very space between (in the case of sounds) is the thing we measure, namely from some beginning to some end. It is in thee, my mind, that I measure times. . . . the impression which things as they pass by cause in thee; remains even when they are gone; this it is which, still present, I measure, not the things which pass by to make this impression. This I measure, when I measure times. Either then this is time, or I do not measure time."
(Paragraph XXVIII)

Augustine recognized clearly that "time" is subjective—that it is a function of nature's "observer", rather than a function of nature herself. Time is an extension of consciousness, for as Augustine says, "It is in thee, my mind, that I measure times." In a universe without a continuing observer, time would be absent.* The same is true of space. Try, if you will, to imagine a world which does not contain an observer. In one sense of course, this is impossible since the very act of imagining a world entails an observer of what is imagined. In this sense therefore there could not be imagination even of a world containing only mass, without also an observer

* This is true not withstanding that other stars and galaxies existed before our own, since we are here speaking of the psychological aspects of time, even though we extrapolate to times when humans did not exist.

16

thereof. Nevertheless, with little effort you can imagine yourself not as a discriminating observer but scanning the world like a new born child, or more accurately, like a camera, without thought, memory or interest—somewhat as one occasionally does absentmindedly. In this situation mass would be apparent as a kind of form but would have no depth. Would one observe in such case anything called space? Does the idea of space not arise only when one is able to perceive, to think about, or to talk of the relation of one portion of the world to another? Does space not require memory of what has been observed in order to make comparisons? In the absence of any observer at all (in the sense I have asked you to imagine) there would be no such thing as space—there would be only mass (although it would be a peculiar kind of mass, possessing form but not substance).*

Enter now upon this scene an observer of the world, one who has memory, but who captures only a fleeting observation. There is to him in retrospect not only form (mass) but that form has structure and location. In short there is space. Now go a little farther. Let this observer have continuity of observation. He will now observe change of the position and structure of mass, that is to say, motion. In short there is time. Space and time it is clear are not attributes of nature, but are qualities imposed upon nature by her observer.[7] This may not be news to a neurologist or psychologist (except as to the manner of its exposition); it is, however, to some scientists and philosophers. Furthermore, it matters not whether we speak of "subjective time" in the sense which Einstein mentions it or time as the fourth dimension, in the sense which physicists themselves use. They are both subjective times. Indeed, the physicist's time is more subjective than egocentric time for it requires not only an "observer" to see it, but one acute enough to utilize the mathematics of physics.

Dymon

But really, you haven't satisfied the curiosity of the layman regarding "creation". What if he *does* understand Darwin and Oparin? What if he *does* understand your comments on "time"?

[7] For a careful analysis of some of these points, see *The Measure of Time* by H. Poincare.

*The perception of mass is itself subject to similar comments. The argument of the solipsists that we cannot know the nature of the physical world because of the unreliability of the senses is for these reasons true but trivial. See "Other Minds", by John Wisdom.

He'll still say, "That's all very well, but how did the earth, the planets and the inorganic matter you speak of get here in the first place?"

Eirat

Certainly he will! But that's another story. There are many accounts of the subject given by astronomers. He certainly should be able to satisfy himself that, on the theory of an expanding universe at any rate, there is a coherent theory of creation. He will see that, if the universe is expanding at a certain rate, that rate being uniformly greater the farther away from us that other galaxies appear, then it is possible to extrapolate back to the commencement of the expansion and by applying the known laws and facts of astronomy and nuclear physics to reconstruct the expansion from the time it began. He will see that possibly due to some prior period of contraction the cosmic masses may have been pressurized into a completely heterogeneous volume of electrons, protons and other nuclear particles. He will see that as the expansion began the elementary particles formed aggregates—prototypes of atomic nuclei, much like a nuclear reaction. He will see, as Gamow says:

"During the earlier period of nuclear cooking, which lasted not more than an hour of time, cosmic space was full of high energy gamma radiation, the mass density of which greatly exceeded the density of ordinary atomic matter. The temperature throughout the universe was in the neighborhood of a billion degrees, but the density of matter was comparable to the density of air at high altitudes. Following that highly productive first hour of our universe, nothing in particular happened for the next 30 million years. The gas, consisting of the newly formed atoms, continued to expand and its temperature became lower and lower. Radiant energy which at the beginning played a predominant role in the evolutionary process, gradually lost its importance and by the end of the thirty-millionth year, yielded its priority in favor of ordinary atomic matter. As soon as matter took over, the force of gravity (speaking of gravity in the Newtonian sense) which represents one of the most important characteristics of ponderable matter, came into play, breaking up the hitherto homogeneous gas into gigantic clouds, the protogalaxies. In that era, the temperature dropped to approximately that which we call 'room temperature', so that space was still rather warm, though completely dark.

While the original proto-galaxies were being driven farther and farther apart by continued expansion, material in their interiors began to con-

18

dense into a multitude of much smaller aggregations called proto-stars. Because of the comparatively small size of these proto-stars their contraction progressed quite rapidly. Very soon the temperature in their interiors reached the value at which nuclear reactions between hydrogen and various light elements would take place, and space became bright again, being illuminated by myriads of stars. When the stars were formed by the condensation of the gaseous material of the proto-galaxies, some of that material was left over in their vicinity and from it sprang planetary systems. The planets were too small to create their own sources of nuclear energy; they cooled off fast and developed solid rocky crusts." [8]

This at any rate, while it does not deal with first and second generation stars and hence glosses over the creation of the heavier elements, is a respectable account of the history of matter on the theory of an expanding universe. "Creation" as used in Gamow's astronomical account certainly does not mean making something out of nothing, as contrasted to both the original and modified theories of Fred Hoyle regarding the continuous creation of matter in intergalactic space.

Dymon

But to make something out of nothing, isn't that just the sense in which people usually speak of creation? They will agree with an account of the creation of matter such as Gamow's and then go on to say, "That's all very well, matter may be nothing but solidified or crystallized energy, so to speak, then who or what created this evolutive ancestor of mass-energy?" All you've said is that once there was a highly concentrated and pressurized volume of energy and then as the energy expanded and cooled into matter it became, over a few hundred million years, the galaxies, the stars and the planets. This doesn't really explain anything about the miracle of "creation". What do you do with this kind of person?

Eirat

Well, it certainly isn't easy, but perhaps we can throw some light on it. What does this person mean when he speaks of the "miracle of creation"?

Dymon

Presumably he means where did the matter or energy or mass-energy, whichever you say came first, come from? A perfectly sensible question, if I may so presume to say.

[8] *The Creation of the Universe,* George Gamow, pages 134–135.

Eirat

But if I may so presume to answer, that is just what he is *not* asking. He's not asking where matter or energy came from. In fact, when he speaks of the miracle of creation he's not asking a question at all. By implication, he's stating a proposition. He's postulating a creator, to create something out of nothing so that he'll have an answer to the question he can't otherwise answer. Creation in this sense is a concept of man's (of the observer). There is no empirical evidence of it in the universe.

Dymon

Well, I must confess that so far I've seen no light.

Eirat

Very well, let's look for it. When a person speaks of the "miracle of creation" he means just what most physicists do *not* mean. He means "making something out of nothing". But what is it to make something out of nothing? What *is* nothing? If asked this question one would probably answer along these lines: "Nothing? Well, it's a bit like a vacuum. It's an absence of matter and an absence of energy. It's just what it says—it's *no thing*."

But isn't that one of our early definitions of "space"? Leibniz said over two hundred years ago that space is simply "the order or relation of things among themselves. Without matter occupying it, it is 'nothing'." And physics has agreed with this.[9] So he who would create something out of nothing would create matter out of empty space (or more accurately, create matter out of empty space-time). Now, how does one create material objects out of space when space itself is only an order or relation of material objects among themselves?[10] The concept "nothing" is meaningless unless we have physical objects with which to begin our definition of it. "Nothing" and "something" are concomitant concepts. It is therefore absurd to speak of creating something out of "nothing".

Dymon

Aren't we back again to the problem of the observer? Someone might dispute your last proposition. He might say, "I can perfectly well envisage a universe with nothing in it and ask how the matter (or the energy) came to be in it."

---

[9] *Space, Time & Gravitation,* Sir Arthur Eddington, page 8: *"Physicist—* the space which you are speaking of must be a sort of abstraction of the extensional relations of matter. *Relativist*—exactly so."
[10] Augustine makes this error in Book 12, *Confessions.*

20

Eirat

Yes, and you know as well as I that the observer in your hypothetical case is made of matter and *he* is in the universe observing its emptiness. So it's not quite empty. Ask him if he can imagine an empty universe in the absence of himself to imagine it. *That* should keep him guessing.

Dymon

I'm not sure it *would* keep him guessing. People sometimes believe some very peculiar things about "empty space". Listen to Irving Adler on the subject of Dirac's equation:

"In 1928 Dirac developed an equation which described correctly the wave and particle properties of the electron. When he solved the equation for the energy of an electron that is not bound to a nucleus in an atom, but is moving freely, he got two sets of answers, one with positive energy, and the other with negative energy. The positive answers were the energy levels belonging to electrons travelling at different speeds. The negative answers were completely unexpected and puzzling. Dirac took it for granted that the equation was correct and was giving him new information that had a real meaning. He made a bold guess at what the negative energies might mean, and his guess turned out to be correct.

Dirac said we should take it for granted that, as his equation says, there are negative as well as positive energy levels for an electron. Then he suggested that under normal conditions, every negative level is already occupied by an electron, and that this normal condition is what we call empty space. Now we know that if an electron on a certain level is given enough additional energy, it can be raised to a higher level. So he predicted that if enough energy is concentrated in a small volume of empty space it may raise an electron from a negative energy level, where it is hidden in empty space, to a positive energy level, where it is visible as an ordinary electron. But when it is raised, the negative level that it occupied becomes vacant and appears as a hole in empty space. His equation predicted that a hole in empty space would have the properties of a particle that has the same mass as an electron but the opposite electrical charge. This positively charged electron is now known as a positron, and is represented by e plus. It is called the antiparticle of the electron. If an electron falls into a hole in empty space, then the empty state of space is restored. This means that if an electron and a positron collide, they destroy each other. When the particles disappear, their combined mass is converted into an equivalent amount of electromagnetic energy. Theory predicts that the energy appears in the form of two gamma ray photons." [11]

[11] *Inside the Nucleus,* Irving Adler, page 80.

21

Eirat

Undoubtedly Dirac's equation says that there are negative as well as positive energy levels for an electron. But was it necessary for him to suggest that under normal conditions *every* negative level is already occupied by an electron and that this condition is what we call "empty space".

True, we now know that the positron which Dirac predicted would appear, does appear when energy is concentrated at a point in empty space. But is it necessary to assume that there must exist at this point in space a hidden electron of negative energy level? Is this not carrying the equivalence of mass and energy to the point of nonsense?

Dirac's theory was useful for the prediction of the positron,[12] but when the positron is discovered, the strict necessity for "holes in empty space" disappears with the knowledge of the pair formation.

That which in his theory was a "hole in empty space" *is* a positron and that which was empty space really *is* empty space.

If theory predicts that upon the collision of an electron and a positron their mass is converted to two gamma ray photons, it also predicts that the energy of two gamma ray photons can be converted to the mass of a positron—electron pair. The "hole in empty space" becomes from the standpoint of modern quantum theory an illogical mathematical fiction. A "hole in empty space" is almost as bad as "creating something out of nothing."

Dymon

Nevertheless, your audience will surely not let you off so lightly. They'll say, "Very well, it may be nonsense to talk of creating 'something' out of 'nothing', nevertheless you still haven't explained where mass-energy came from."

Eirat

Yes, they might say something like that; they might not see the similarity between "creating something out of nothing" and "asking where mass-energy came from."

Dymon

Is there such a similarity?

[12] It has later been useful also in the prediction of the Lamb shift in the spectrum of atomic hydrogen from the vacuum fluctuations and polarization effects.

Eirat

You know very well there is. Let us examine the question, "Where did mass-energy come from?" In the first place, when we ask this question do we expect an answer in terms of a *location?* By that I mean this: If we have a theory of the observable universe and we ask where that universe came from, would we be satisfied with an answer which said, "Oh, it came from a distance twice its diameter removed in the direction of the Hydra galaxy." Obviously not—and the reason why such an answer would be unsatisfactory is that when we ask where mass-energy came from we are thinking of the mass-energy of all the universe. We've really incorporated another notion in the question, namely, not only all of mass-energy but all of space-time.

Dymon

I see what you mean—we draw a mental circle around all of space-time and with reference to all of the mass-energy therein we ask "Where did it come from?" We don't expect an answer in terms of a location *outside* the circle since our circle already comprises all of space-time. We're asking how it was created within the circle. How was it created from nothing? And this is your similarity between "asking where mass-energy came from" and "creating something out of nothing."

Eirat

Precisely—and with the latter question we're back to the problem of "nothing". These questions make no sense. "Nothing" is like a "circle" or a "square root"—it is a useful, logical construction, but it makes no more sense for mass-energy to come from "nothing" than it does for it to come from a "circle", a "square root" or the "back of a turtle".

Dymon

What you say is true, but do you really expect to convince the mystic of this? You are not manifesting the religious impulse, which is so important to him, when you look about you and say, "Where did all of this come from?" To the religious person there is amazement, humility and beauty in this question.

Eirat

I realize that. I am not devoid of feeling. I look about me and I too feel the amazement, the humility and the beauty but they are in the observation, not in the question.

Dymon

True, true! But I'm afraid your critic would not yield so easily. He'd say, "You insist that to create something out of 'nothing' is meaningless but is that true? If space is finite, that is to say it comes to an end somewhere, surely beyond that is a 'nothing' from which matter could have come."

Eirat

I'll try to answer your critic. He has gone part way with the physicist but not very far. We shall have to see how far he's gone before answering. Take as a start the Newtonian concept of space and matter. Newton pictured the universe as comprised of matter scattered throughout a vast area of space—with the space going on to infinity in all directions. It was thought by him that the universe had to be infinite. If it were not, one would have to explain what lay beyond any arbitrary finite boundary. But even on this theory an infinite universe could not contain a uniform distribution of matter.* If it did, the mass of the universe would be infinite, and more important, there would be an infinite amount of light. Obviously however, mass and light were not infinite. If they were, the heavens instead of being dark would be uniformly bright. Also, a uniform distribution of matter was contrary to what was actually observed by the telescopes of a later day, still peering into space in accordance with Newton's laws. Matter was not uniformly distributed. Quite the contrary. When other galaxies besides our own Milky Way were observed it soon became apparent that numerous though they may be they were spread sparingly in space. An island universe it was called. But the amount of matter such a universe held, if its space were considered to be infinite, was so small that the laws governing the movements of galaxies would long ago have ensured their dispersal, leaving as a residue a relatively empty and unoccupied universe. Such then was the situation which Einstein examined. The Newtonian concept of infinite space contained too many contradictions.[13] In Einstein's opinion the difficulty lay in

---

* It should not be thought that Newton himself believed the distribution of matter to be even. He said, "If matter were evenly distributed throughout an infinite space . . . some of it would convene into one mass and some into another, so as to make an infinite number of great masses, scattered great distances from one another throughout all that infinite space. And thus might the sun and stars be formed."

[13] Newtonian cosmologies do not necessarily have *all* the contradictions mentioned here. See H. Bondi, *Cosmology*.

Newton's assumption that the geometry of space was Euclidean.*

Euclid's geometry worked perfectly well on earth but was it true of space? As Eddington has since stated:

"Supposing that one corner of a triangle was in a very intense gravitational field—far stronger than any we have had experience of—I have good ground for believing that under those conditions you might find the sum of two sides of a triangle, as measured with a rigid rod, appreciably less than the third side. In that case would you be prepared to give up Euclidean geometry?" [14]

For these and other reasons, Einstein concluded that space was not infinite and further that Euclidean geometry did not prevail in it.**

Believing as he did that a gravitational field is governed by the amount of mass and the velocity of that mass in it, he concluded that the geometry of space must be dependent upon its gravitational structure, that is, upon the total amount of matter in it. If there were a gravitational distortion of space in the vicinity of matter so that in effect other objects ran downhill towards that matter, then the more matter there were in the universe the more curvature there would be of space. Obviously, if space were curved because of the matter in it, that curve must either be open like a parabola or hyperbola, or closed like a sphere. The available evidence seems to favor a closed curve. Therefore, space-time, if it is a four dimensional *closed* curve, is finite. Its size can be calculated if one knows the curvature. It's a four dimensional sphere.† Various estimates of size have in fact been made. The curvature or gravitational distortion being dependent upon the amount of matter, if the average density of matter in the universe can be ascertained, the degree of curvature and hence the size of the universe can be calculated. Astronomers having made what appear to be reasona-

[14] *Space, Time & Gravitation,* Sir Arthur Eddington, page 5. (Eddington is, of course, assuming that the rod does not shrink).

* This was Einstein's general theory. In his special theory he used Euclidean geometry.

** I am indebted to Lincoln Barnett for the format of this paragraph.

† Gamow has suggested that if galaxies wane in intrinsic brightness by only a few percent in a billion years we'll have to reverse this conclusion. Space would in such event be in an open curve such as a parabola or hyperbola. However, James Scott of Ottawa contends that the general theory of relativity is wrong regarding *any* curvature of space-time. He says that although light may be curved by a gravitational field, its speed remains unaffected. We may soon know which is correct.

ble estimates of the average density of matter in space in terms of grams per cubic centimeter, the curvature was determined, and thus the radius of the universe has been estimated at about 13 billion light years.[15]

Hence, we are now after this lengthy preamble, at the first stage of our critic's reasoning. He says, "If the universe, including space, is finite, then beyond that must be a nothing from which matter could have come." In saying this, our critic has ignored the other aspect of our spatial geometry. The universe is not only finite we said, but unbounded. There is nothing very mysterious about that statement. The surface of a balloon is finite, but unbounded for an insect restricted to travelling thereon. He can go in any direction as far as he likes and his universe in unbounded. It is nevertheless, finite. Space-time in four dimensions is similar to that. We can go as far as we like in any direction without being bounded but our universe is still finite. Our space comes back on itself in a closed curve.[16] So our critic cannot look *outside* at some area not included in the universe. Everywhere he goes or looks is *in* the universe. We must therefore be careful in making statements like "beyond that is nothing" because the "beyond" is not one which we can, even in imagination, look at or travel to. Similarly, one should be careful not to take too literally the analogy of a sphere as the shape of the universe. A more accurate three dimensional analogy would be a balloon which has burst. It has burst because light is now unable to travel around it. At one time presumably, light could travel around the universe. Now, however, the rate of expansion of the universe is too rapid to permit it. Light, despite its tremendous velocity, is too slow to complete a lap of the track because the track is expanding faster than light can run.[17] With these facts in mind, it can be seen that if our critic says, "Beyond space-time is a nothing from which matter could have come," he is not expressing a criticism. The "nothing" he speaks of is the same kind of "nothing" as that which comprises space—only it hasn't got matter imbedded in it. Therefore, if he suggests that matter or energy were created from this "nothing", he's making the same

[15] Undoubtedly its radius will change with better quasar detection.

[16] Although the idea of a closed universe in which one might see a single object such as a quasar, by looking in opposite directions now seems improbable.

[17] *The Expanding Universe,* Sir Arthur Eddington.

type of error he made in supposing earlier that matter could have been created from the "nothing" which is space. The fact which some people overlook is that they, the observers, and indeed everyone and everything else are *inside* the four dimensional space-time framework which physics utilizes to describe the universe.*

Dymon

How do you mean that some people overlook this fact? In what way is it overlooked?

Eirat

Well, the problem of "creation" is twofold, as we have seen. One part comprises the logical confusion which surrounds creation at the "beginning". The other is the logical confusion which surrounds creation of "something" out of "nothing". In the first case, as we have seen, a statement about the "beginning of time" involves trying to say something about the time axis of our four dimensional reference system in language which we normally use for describing phenomena *within* that reference system. In the second case, a statement about "creating something out of nothing" involves trying to say something about mass-energy in terms of that which is simply the relation of one portion of mass-energy to another, that is to say, space. Space-time is our reference system; four dimensional geometry is the deductive system we utilize to describe the space-time co-ordinates, and mass-energy is the phenomenon we describe. The confusion surrounding both aspects of creation stems from the failure to recognize these simple propositions.

Dymon

Perhaps everyone, including Newton, was guilty of this confusion before Einstein, but is the mistake still made?

Eirat

It is not only made. I've never seen it *not* made, except in the purest empirical writings. Consider the following passage from a well-known writer:

"Everything indeed, everything visible in nature or established in

---

* Similar considerations to those contained in this paragraph would apply if space were found to be either negatively curved or flat, since such considerations arise not from the general but from the special theory of relativity. Basically, that which is overlooked is that the observer as well as that which is observed are within the four dimensional continuum.

theory, suggests that the universe is implacably progressing toward final darkness and decay.

There is an important philosophical corollary to this view. For if the universe is running down and nature's processes are proceeding in just one direction, the inseparable inference is that everything had a *beginning;* somehow and sometime the cosmic processes were started, the stellar fires ignited, and the whole vast pageant of the universe brought into being. Most of the clues, moreover, that have been discovered at the inner and outer frontiers of scientific cognition suggest a definite time of Creation. The unvarying rate at which uranium expends its nuclear energies and the absence of any natural process leading to its formation indicates that all the uranium on earth must have come into existence at one specific time, which, according to the best calculations of geophysicists, was about two billion years ago. The tempo at which the wild thermonuclear processes in the interiors of stars transmute matter into radiation enables astronomers to compute with fair assurance the duration of stellar life, and the figure they reach as the likely age of most stars visible in the firmament today is two billion years. The arithmetic of the geophysicists and astrophysicists is thus in striking agreement with that of the cosmogonists who, basing their calculations on the apparent velocity of the receding galaxies, find that the universe began to expand two billion years ago. And there are other signs in other areas of science that submit the same reckoning. So all the evidence that points to the ultimate annihilation of the universe points just as definitely to an inception fixed in time.

Even if one acquiesces to the idea of an immortal pulsating universe, within which the sun and earth and super-giant red stars are comparative newcomers, the problem of initial origin remains. It merely pushes the time of Creation into the infinite past. For while theorists have adduced mathematically impeccable accounts of the fabrication of galaxies, stars, star dust; atoms and even of the atom's components, every theory rests ultimately on the a priori assumption that *something* was already in existence—whether free neutrons, energy quanta, or simply the blank inscrutable 'world stuff', the cosmic essence, of which the multifarious universe was subsequently wrought." [18]

It is significant that the only two italicized words in this passage are those we have described as containing logical confusion.

The author says firstly that the "universe is implacably progressing towards final darkness and decay." This means, of course, only that the second law of Thermodynamics is operating in the universe. But possibly this law is a corollary of the *expansion* of

[18] *The Universe and Dr. Einstein,* Lincoln Barnett, pages 115-116.

28

the universe. If the universe were contracting the second law of Thermodynamics might possibly be reversed. The author also takes as a philosophical corollary of the universe running down that "everything had a beginning." The only "beginning" in the narrative he has considered is from the calculated commencement of the expansion of the universe. The writer, however, says "The stellar fires ignited and the whole vast pageant of the universe *brought into being*." He speaks of a "definite *time of creation*" (my italics) and concluded that "the evidence that points to the ultimate annihilation of the universe points just as definitely to an inception fixed in time." True, it points to a time of commencement of the expansion of matter and possibly to a time of running down but *not* to a time of either creation or annihilation. We know that the farthest galaxies are now receding at speeds relative to us of the order of one-half the speed of light.[19] Who is to say the expansion will not stop? He then speaks of the time of creation, even on the theory of a pulsating universe, only being pushed farther into the past.* But this only illustrates the logical confusion of "beginning" which we have discussed. The author complains that creation is pushed farther into the past, but does nothing to clarify the confusion. He says that "every theory rests ultimately on the a priori assumption that *something* was already in existence". But of course it does! Here is a classic example of the other aspect of logical confusion, namely, the creation of "something out of nothing".[20] Further, there is nothing a priori about the assumption at all. It is the best founded empirical assumption one can think of.

Dymon

But the quotation you are criticizing is one from a writer attempting to popularize science. Would you find such statements made by a purely empirical scientist?

[19] It has been suggested by the astronomer, Schmidt of California, that the quasar 3C-9 is receding at 80% of the speed of light. And Dr. Shuter of U.B.C. has shown that the quasar 3C-147 is very likely outside our own galaxy.
[20] Augustine makes the mistake of creating something out of nothing, paragraphs 6, 7, 8 and 22, Book 12, *Confessions*.
* Gamow has pointed out that the pulsating theory requires a total mass in intergalactic space more than seven times that of the galaxies. This seems unlikely.

Eirat

Would you agree with the classification of Sir Arthur Eddington as a purely empirical astronomer? The following quotation, when he talks about his subject, does not appear free from the logical confusion we have described.

"The beginning seems to present insuperable difficulties unless we agree to look on it as frankly supernatural. We may have to let it go at that. But I have referred elsewhere to the danger of limiting scientific investigation to a bounded domain. Instead of honestly facing the intricacies of our problem, we may be led to think its difficulties have been solved when they have only been swept over the boundary. Sweeping them back and back, the pile increases until it forms an unclimbable barrier. Perhaps it is this barrier that we call 'the beginning'." [21]

Eddington at least suspects that there is something wrong with "creation" and "beginning" but apparently hasn't any idea of what it is.

Dymon

I am satisfied. You haven't really answered the question, but after listening to your analysis I no longer feel inclined to ask it.

Eirat

That is all any philosopher can hope for. Philosophy, after all, is not a subject, it is an activity.

Dymon

So far we have talked briefly of the evolution of life from inorganic matter, of space and time and of cosmology. Should we not be able to draw some ethical conclusions from all of this?

Eirat

It never ceases to astonish me that the moment people gain some scientific knowledge, and in particular biological knowledge, they attempt to hang an ethical theory on it. Herbert Spencer did it, and more recently Lecomte DuNouy has tried it.

Man naturally tries to develop a "Weltanschauung" but people would do well, if they insist upon developing naturalistic ethical theories, to read G. E. Moore. Listen to what he said as early as 1903 about evolutionary ethics.

[21] *The Expanding Universe* by Sir Arthur Eddington, page 125. Howard Robertson makes the same mistake as Eddington when he asks, "Did the universe originate at some finite time in the past, or has it existed forever? The question may not be one for science alone to answer . . ." (Scientific American 1957)

30

"Among attempts to systemise an appeal to nature, that which is now most prevalent is to be found in the application to ethical questions of the term 'Evolution'—in the ethical doctrines which have been called 'Evolutionistic'. These doctrines are those which maintain that the course of 'evolution' while it shews us the direction in which we are developing, thereby and for that reason shews us the direction in which we ought to develop.

The modern vogue of 'evolution' is chiefly owing to Darwin's investigations as to the origin of species. Darwin formed a strictly biological hypothesis as to the manner in which certain forms of animal life became established, while others died out and disappeared. His theory was that this might be accounted for, partly at least in the following way. When certain varieties occurred (the cause of their occurrence is still, in the main, unknown), it might be that some of the points in which they varied from their parent species or from other species then existing, made them better able to persist in the environment in which they found themselves—less liable to be killed off. They might, for instance, be better able to endure the cold or heat or changes of the climate; better able to find nourishment from what surrounded them; better able to escape from or resist other species which fed upon them; better fitted to attract or to master the other sex. Being thus less liable to die, their numbers relatively to other species would increase; and that very increase in their numbers might tend towards the extinction of those other species. This theory, to which Darwin gave the name 'Natural Selection', was also called the theory of survival of the fittest. The natural process which it thus described was called evolution. It was very natural to suppose that evolution meant evolution from what was lower into what was higher; in fact it was observed that at least one species, commonly called higher—the species man—had so survived, and among men again it was supposed that the higher races, ourselves for example, had shewn a tendency to survive the lower, such as the North American Indians. We can kill them more easily than they can kill us. The doctrine of evolution was then represented as an explanation of how the higher species survives the lower. Spencer for example, constantly uses 'more evolved' as equivalent to 'higher'. But it is to be noted that this forms no part of Darwin's scientific theory. That theory will explain, equally well, how by an alteration in the environment (the gradual cooling of the earth, for example) quite a different species from man, a species which we think infinitely lower, might survive us. The survival of the fittest does not mean, as one might suppose, the survival of what is fittest to fulfil a good purpose—best adapted to a good end; at the last, it means merely the survival of the fittest to survive; and the value of the scientific theory, and it is a theory of great value, just consists in shewing what are the causes which produce certain biological effects. Whether these effects are good or bad, it cannot pretend to judge." [22]

Dymon

Then what about Albert Schweitzer's outlook—specifically his "reverence for life" ethic—was this too based upon evolutionary considerations?

Eirat

I don't know what it *was* based upon, apart from his consideration of the historical Jesus, but it certainly could have been based upon evolutionary theory. If one recognizes the evolution and interdependence of species one couldn't fail to recognize one's own close kinship to an animal, a tree, or a plant. Schweitzer's moral appeared to be to treat all of life with reverence because of this kinship. It may be that one should do this, but I'm at a loss to see the empirical basis for stopping there. We've already seen how, on Oparin's theory, organic matter arose from the inorganic, so if kinship is the criterion for reverence one must extend it to include reverence also for basalt rocks and inorganic salts. Cosmology shows us that we and the stars, the plants and nebulae, gamma rays and mountain streams are all made of the same stuff. This would logically extend such reverence to include not only life but the whole of the universe. It would appear therefore that to base an ethic such as Schweitzer's upon evolution is not only faulty in the manner that Moore suggests but extending it to accord with organic evolution renders it meaningless. The reverence as Schweitzer described it is perhaps nothing more than understanding the universe to the best of one's ability.

Dymon

I'm not sure I can agree with that statement. I think we should examine "reverence" a little more carefully. Reverence was in man long before science extended his understanding. But man has always sought a rational basis for his reverence. It seems to me that if one wishes properly to understand "reverence" one should investigate the relation between the language of religion and the language of physics. Such investigation might throw new light on the concept "reverence".

Eirat

Well, I can see one objection to begin with. Firstly, "God" to

[22] *Principia Ethica,* Cambridge University Press, page 47.

those theologians who still use the concept means something more than the "universe" means to the physicist. We have already discussed "creation of something out of nothing". Nevertheless, when the theologian speaks of God, his concept is not limited to the physical universe. Say what you like, he has in mind a being outside of space, time, mass and energy. What that is supposed to mean, I don't know but that's what he *says* he has in mind.

Dymon

If this be so, then "God" by definition included neither space, time, mass nor energy. God is then remote and banished beyond the realm of physics; his influence too would be so remote as not to merit consideration.

Eirat

How then connect physics with religion?

Dymon

Well, first of all, is the theologian really saying only that God is outside space, time, matter and energy? I don't think so. He would dispute your statement and say that God is not only outside of but is within space-time and mass-energy. What can we conclude from this? Firstly, we can say that this idea is not to be confused with physical concepts. Secondly, we should take his statement in two parts, namely, the idea of a God being outside the world as one part and the idea of a God being inside as the other part and look at each of these to see if they resemble the concepts of physics or indeed if they are meaningful. Taking the first part, what is the theologian saying when he says that God is outside of and transcends all of space-time and mass-energy? He can't be saying anything about the universe; if he were, he wouldn't use religious language, he'd use physical language.

Eirat

Pardon the interruption, but surely you've heard it suggested that God is an hypothesis unnecessary to science.[23]

Dymon

I agree, but we are not now talking exclusively of science.

Eirat

That may be so, but presumably you've also examined the analysis of the logical positivists to the effect that the statement,

[23] T. H. Huxley.

"God exists", is the same kind of statement as "God does not exist"; namely, a meaningless one. It is said that not only can no one prove which of these statements is correct but that neither statement tells us anything—that there is no verification technique for proving either of them right or wrong, or indeed, for showing either of them to be meaningful.

Dymon

Certainly, I've read and participated in these analyses and there's a great deal to be said in their favor. As you know, they extend David Hume's attitude that metaphysical propositions are nonsense.

Eirat

Why then do you dignify these statements with discussion?

Dymon

Because, my dear fellow, as I said before, man has always sought a rational basis for his reverence and it would not do, arrogantly to dismiss the theologian's concept simply because physics and philosophy do not use them.

Eirat

But really, the word "God" is fraught with emotional connotations of every conceivable kind and description. Would you not do better to avoid it if you seek to be rational?

Dymon

I can only state that emotional connotations hardly form a basis for ignoring concepts that occupy the time and mental energy of a great portion of the world's population.

Eirat

You are then equating intellectual attainment with majority rule.

Dymon

Perhaps I am—if so, please bear with me a few moments. I do not believe that the word "God" has the variable meaning you suggest, nor do I believe, like the positivists, that it is devoid of meaning, nor do I, like some scientists, believe that it is an unnecessary hypothesis. I do agree that there are valid criticisms of most other religious words, such as "soul", "heaven", "hell", "hereafter", etc.—and we've seen some of these criticisms. They are like the criticisms of psychological entities—and valid in the same way and only to the same extent. The conventional ecclesiastical language and theological categories have of course become meaningless, but perhaps God is not as dead as he seems. Certainly, however, the immature concepts of him have failed to survive. The so-called "death of God" theologians [24] appear to have two things in common.

Firstly, they say that talk of a divine or otherwise supernatural force is meaningless and irrelevant because that kind of "God language" is not related to contemporary experience. In this, of course, they are correct—they are fifty years behind everyone else in this regard, but nonetheless correct.

Secondly, they affirm that the secular world is the source of all spiritual and ethical, as well as physical, standards. In this I think that they are only partly correct for reasons I will mention later. However that may be, as a mistaken consequence of both these views they apparently choose to reject God and to deify Jesus. It seems to have escaped their notice that Jesus when faced with this choice made the opposite decision. He chose "God" over himself. And he willingly went to his death as a consequence of that choice.

Eirat

I see no great quarrel with those comments. Indeed, I have some ideas of my own on the subject but let us get on with our investigation. We won't get any help in this from the "death of God" theologians. You were asking, what is the conventional theologian saying when he says that God is outside of space-time and mass-energy? I should be very surprised if he's saying anything at all.

Dymon

I don't think you *would* be surprised. After all, imagine yourself talking to a visitor from another planet who has never heard the word "God" and has no equivalent in his vocabulary. This in itself is a difficult feat of imagination. To have a visitor from another planet seems much less unlikely in itself than to have such a visitor who has no equivalent for "God" in his vocabulary. Nevertheless, presuppose such a visitor asking you what the word "God" meant in your language. Would you tell him it was an unnecessary hypothesis? Would you say it was a meaningless word? Would you

[24] Thomas J. Alitzer of Emory University, Atlanta, Ga., William H. Hamilton of the Colgate, Rochester, N.Y. Divinity School, and Paul Van Buren of Temple University, Philadelphia, Pa.

say, "Oh, it's a primitive conception of a deity"? If the latter, he would of course ask you what a deity was. Let us suppose further that our visitor had a good vocabulary of physics. What would you tell him?

Eirat

I would beg the question. I would say that since he has no such word in his vocabulary he's better off without it.

Dymon

But if you do that, he, being a questioning fellow, would want to know why he's better off. You'd have to face up to it. You'd probably start with an historic preamble, would you not? You'd say that in the infancy of man he was able to discern few physical principles—that Cromagnon and Neanderthal man thought there was a fire god, a wind god, a spirit of the mountains, a spirit of the waters. The Egyptians and Aztecs and even Ulysses, spoke of sun gods. There was a diversity of Gods for every startling or awe-inspiring physical phenomenon which impinged upon man's consciousness. Early men were on familiar terms with fire. Yet there was a God *behind* and *in* the fire manifesting himself by means of the fire.

Similarly with early sun gods, serpent gods, gods of bulls and gods of war. The symbols were manifestations of the power. Man was fearful and reverent before the unknown powers. As his knowledge increased his choice of gods became more sophisticated. The Greeks had only a few gods, all of whom had homes on Mount Olympus. The fierce Jehovah supplanted the indolent, quarrelsome and fun-loving gods of the Romans and the North Europeans. With Christianity a single God was established in Europe. Beyond doubt, man has always used the idea of a God or a spirit to signify his reverence for that which his knowledge does not encompass. Philosophers, although later in the cultural evolution, did a similar thing when they looked for "the being behind the manifestations" or "reality" or the "real world" as opposed to "the chaotic and treacherous impressions of the senses". From Plato to Kant they were concerned with "the prison house of the senses". Philosophical doubt is possibly epitomized by Descartes who, when pressed to justify the evidence of his senses, defiantly said, "I think, therefore I am."

The quest for knowledge then has gone hand in hand with the quest for the "spirit", the "ultimate reality", or "God". And really, is the primitive man looking for the God behind the fire or the rocks, any different from a modern theologian looking for God behind space-time and mass-energy? Primitive man knew that what he understood was not the whole story and he was reverent towards what to him was unknown or unknowable. Are modern man's reasons for reverence less compelling than those of his primitive forebears? With some such preamble as the foregoing I think you'd set about explaining "God" to our visitor.

Eirat

Yes, I think I would, but in view of our friend's imagined vocabulary of physics, I'd be most embarrassed if he began to examine me on the concept.

Dymon

But is there any reason why you *should* be embarrassed? He who has believed in God throughout man's history has at least been consistent. God to him has always been behind or outside of the known physical world just as to the classical theologian God is outside of space-time. The chief difference is that primitive man believed in the direct intervention of his deity in earthly affairs. Sophisticated clerics no longer believe in miracles which contravene physical laws. In the first place, they are unnecessary and in the second place they are not nearly so miraculous as the natural truth.

Eirat

But good heavens—here you are allowing phrases like "outside of space-time" to be bandied about when not long ago you agreed with me that they were nonsense.

Dymon

And so they are—if one is trying to make a rational factual statement, but is that what a theologian is doing? Really, my dear fellow, if the believer's God existed in the same sense that my pen does, such existence would have been accepted without question long ago by all men.

Eirat

Then God is a bit of a poltergeist, slipping through the interstices of space like the 19th century ether waves. Surely God is a meaningless figment of man's imagination. Surely man created God and not vice-versa.

Dymon

Certainly man created God—in the mental sense, but he also

37

created "time", "electron", "four" and "square root" in a similar sense. Science creates new concepts as the need arises and discards the old. Religion on the other hand keeps the same concept but alters its meaning to accord with advances in knowledge. It is often said that religion and science do not conflict because they speak different languages. This of course is not true. They often have conflicted in the past and on each occasion religion has had to adjust to account for the increase in knowledge. But is this so remarkable? Science is constantly adjusting; why shouldn't religion? The theologian is properly criticized as reactionary if his dogma remains dogma; that is to say, if his concepts fail to keep pace with developments which require their adjustment. So is the scientist.

Eirat

All that you've said so far is that science can tolerate religion, so long as religion learns its proper place and does not purport to make factual statements about the universe. This viewpoint envisages two classes of people, scientists on the one hand and theologians on the other. But what of the scientist-theologian; are there such?

Dymon

There are! Witness what Einstein once said:

"To know that what is impenetrable to us really exists, manifesting itself as the highest wisdom and the most radiant beauty which our dull faculties can comprehend only in their most primitive forms—this knowledge, this feeling, is at the centre of true religiousness." [25]

Here then is a physical theoretician who unravelled some of the puzzles of the universe saying that much of the universe is "impenetrable" to us and that we comprehend it only in primitive form. If that be so then that portion of the universe which has *not* been comprehended in the sense of being explicable on scientific theory is to Einstein a proper sphere to attribute to God. Obviously, as soon as it is explained, it comes out of the impenetrable and into the realm of physics.

Eirat

Have you then relegated God to the area of the impenetrable? As you know, that area is encroached upon by science every day.

[25] *The Universe and Dr. Einstein,* Lincoln Barnett.

38

Dymon

No, I haven't; I've simply tried to explain what the classical theologian is saying when he says that God is beyond space-time. He's not making a factual statement. In fact he may even have chosen a poor analogy. If he'd said that God was behind metric-gravitational space or electromagnetic space the physicist might be more apt to believe him—for connecting these two has been a problem area.

Eirat

God is becoming more shy, is he? As knowledge progresses, he's hiding himself more and more?

Dymon

Quite the contrary! You recall our theologian saying that not only is God *outside* the universe but *inside* also? Well, he means that what we see around us and understand to be acting in accordance with physical laws is the manifestation of God. God to him is not a capricious old man sitting on a cloud manipulating the world with puppet strings. If the concept means anything at all, God acts within and by means of the physical laws which we know—so says the classical theologian.

Eirat

It would be appalling to think that there might be two unrelated systems of laws governing the universe: One physical and the other divine.

Dymon

Exactly—the idea is preposterous.

Eirat

How then does one describe God?

Dymon

One doesn't—don't you see that if God were capable of description or representation he would not be God but something else, namely, a subject for physics, biology, cosmology or some other factual discipline, or in the alternative, the totality of these. It has often seemed strange to me that a scientist who is oriented towards religion will, like Lecomte DuNouy, look for a lack of completeness and homogeneity of scientific ideas for confirmation of the existence of God whereas the irreligious scientist like T. H. Huxley, who may be aware of these same deficiencies, will exhibit a faith in their ultimate resolution which could only be based on an idea similar to that of God.

Eirat

I'm not sure I follow you.

Dymon

Well, if you are familiar with DuNouy's thesis, you will notice that he sees evidence of the existence of God in what he thinks is the opposition of evolution to the second law of thermodynamics.

One formulation of this law states that for an isolated material system the thermodynamic entropy does not decrease.[26] Every successive state entails either an increase in its entropy or no change thereto. Hence its irreversibility and its trend to an ever increasing symmetry and levelling of energy. DuNouy suggests that adaptation, natural selection and mutation of amorphous living matter has produced a systematic *increase* in biological dissymetries both structural and functional culminating in man, and that this exhibits a trend contrary to the second law of thermodynamics. I do not agree. There never has, in the history of evolution on earth, been an isolated material system—always the sun has provided an outside source of radiant energy. Far from being an isolated system, radiant energy bombarded the infant earth and the entire mechanism of photosynthesis was developed to utilize this energy. Evolution has utilized tremendous *increases* in energy, but virtually all of them have been obtained from the sun. DuNouy says:

"This trend (meaning the evolutionary trend) can hardly be attributed to a rare fluctuation destined to be ironed out statistically, as it has manifested itself steadily for over one thousand million years (probable age of life on this globe), and as the dissymetries, gloriously unconcerned about the law set by man (the 2nd law of thermodynamics), became greater as eons passed by, they culminated in the brain of man." [27]

Certainly this trend has been manifest over the age of life on the globe! During the same period, billions of tons of mass have poured out of the sun in the form of radiation onto the same globe. (3.9×10^{30} Kilogram-calories in 3 billion years). This proves only that the globe where evolution has occurred is not an isolated physical system. It does not show that the trend of evolution is contrary to the 2nd law of thermodynamics.[28]

[26] If the system is prepared in a pure quantum state the entropy remains constant.

[27] *Human Destiny*, page 40.

[28] For a detailed treatment of the role of the 2nd law of thermodynamics in evolution, see *Time's Arrow and Evolution* by Harold F. Blum.

40

To find evidence of God in this trend in the manner of DuNouy is not astute theology. It is bad physics. He is, as we mentioned, looking for two sets of laws, one physical, the other divine. No one disputes that the "rare fluctuation" would most certainly disappear if the sun did. DuNouy then was looking for conflicts of science to prove the existence of God. Certainly many scientific mysteries do exist but is this state of affairs proof of the existence of God? To me the whole approach is wrong.

I prefer to accept the opposite view—the one which has motivated even the irreligious scientist—faith in the underlying unity of nature. Huxley had as much of this faith as anyone else. If the scientist hadn't this faith, he could not function. Above all, the scientist believes that nature exists in a state of statistical order and uniformity.

He believes that the structure of the universe is so ordered and uniform as to be capable of description in terms of the most ordered system ever devised by the mind of man, namely, mathematics. This fact so impressed Einstein that he once said:

"That deeply emotional conviction of a superior reasoning power which is revealed in the incomprehensible universe, forms my idea of God." [29]

He was like a person who finds a watch on the road and says, "Someone made this!"

Eirat

Yes, but unlike the man who finds the watch there is no verification technique for the theologian attempting to prove the proposition that a superior reasoning power exists—nor indeed for proving that the atheist is right either when he denies the same proposition.

Dymon

Is that true? The watch-finder may never have seen a watch before. Let us assume he had not. His judgement is then based upon the appearance of the watch—the regular shape of the parts, the characteristic signs of manufacture, the label on it—all of these indicate to him fabrication by a human being. The verification technique assumes that on the basis of this empirical evidence, the watch-finder can confirm or deny his statement that "someone made this." For this reason his statement is admitted to be a sensible one—the criterion of sense being that its truth or falsity

29 *The Universe and Dr. Einstein*, Lincoln Barnett.

can be verified. It may seem absurd to attempt to confirm a statement of the kind we have chosen, so for the purpose of our analogy, let us imagine that our fine modern Swiss watch is found by an illiterate 8th century peasant or a pygmy of some remote tribe. The question might then be significant. He might easily wonder if the watch had, in fact, been made by man or was it perhaps a ticking clam with limbs inside a transparent shell? The verification technique he pursued would then depend upon the state of his knowledge. The question would be one of evidence—one of relating the watch characteristics with his knowledge of typical characteristics of fabrication. He might even conclude that the watch was too finely made to have been constructed by man. That, for our purpose, is irrelevant. The point is that he would attempt to verify the truth or falsity of the statement "someone made this watch" by empirical evidence within his knowledge. What then is the physicist-theologian saying when he says that the incomprehensible universe reveals to him a superior reasoning power? Can this be verified in the same way that the watch-finder's statement can?

Eirat

You know full well it cannot.

Dymon

It cannot be verified in the sense that someone seeks out a superior reasoning power and obtains from him an admission of his existence, but certainly it is not the case that the proposition is senseless. We haven't the direct testimony of the superior reasoning power but to the physicist-theologian there is a strong circumstantial case.

Eirat

I'd like you to note, however, that Einstein suggested that his conviction was an emotional one.

Dymon

So he did, but is that not something of a contradiction of terms? The conviction, I think, is said by him to be emotional because it cannot be described in mathematical language, but is the conviction less valid for all that? Mathematical propositions, as we know, cannot be confuted by experience because in themselves they tell us nothing about nature. Two plus two is equal to four because it is implicit in the definition of four that two plus two shall be equal to it. As Frege, Russell, Whitehead and Wittgenstein have shown,

42

the same is true of all mathematical and logical propositions. Moreover, they can be deduced from a small number of assumptions. Mathematical conviction then is strong because it tells us nothing we didn't already know, were we only astute enough to see it. Given the assumptions of a deductive system, for example Euclidean geometry, all of the theorems flow from it with certitude simply because they were there all the time. To a more powerful mind than the average mathematician's, simply to state the assumptions would be to state the theorems which are implicit in them. We appear to "discover" mathematical truths only because our minds are not good enough to see at a glance all of the ramifications of the assumptions the moment they are stated. Once discovered, we realize that they *were* implicit all the time. I suggest, therefore, that Einstein need not have qualified his conviction on the ground that it was not purely mathematical. It was quite likely an empirical conviction based upon experience.

Eirat

How so?

Dymon

Well, as we mentioned, it's a question of evidence. I can very well understand someone who spent a lifetime examining the natural sciences, and physics in particular, coming to the conclusion that the universe reveals a superior reasoning power, without being fully conscious of how he reached that conclusion.

Eirat

Footprints on the sands of time?

Dymon

Something like that. After all, the physicist uses the language of mathematics. He measures things and observes their mathematical relations. That's what distinguishes him from others. He doesn't simply say, "It's hot in here." He says, "The temperature is 85 degrees Fahrenheit." When he uses mathematics then, his propositions become meaningful because he is saying that physical phenomena behave in accordance with the mathematical propositions he describes to us. For example, he sometimes says that if E means energy in ergs and M means mass in grams and C means velocity of light in centimetres per second, then E equals MC^2. This is an empirical proposition described in the language of mathematics. And because we are familiar with the deductive system of which equations such as this form part, namely, algebra, we know that if this proposition be true, it is also the case that certain other empirical propositions are true, namely, that $M = E/C^2$ and that $C = \sqrt{\frac{E}{M}}$. In other words, the last two propositions are implicit in the first by virtue of an algebraic deductive system.

Now, one of the avowed aims of science is to be able to deduce the greatest number of physical facts from the least number of general laws. In little more than a lifetime all of the world's substances were reduced to something in excess of 92 elements, and these elements shown to be various aggregates of a few fundamental particles. The atom has become reasonably well understood and its nucleus discovered to be a complex of several distinct entities. At the same time, heat, light, X-rays, radio waves, gamma rays and others were shown to be electromagnetic waves of different length and frequency. We have already noted the equivalence of mass and energy and the quasi-equivalence of space and time.

All of this, remember, was done in the language of mathematics, or shall we say would be meaningless except in terms of mathematics.

The physicist-theologian who says then that the universe evidences a superior reasoning power is saying, I think, that he believes the structure of the universe to be analogous to that of a deductive system and that he, through his intellect and experimental technique, is able occasionally to "discover" truths about that system. But the only deductive systems known to man are those constructed by reasoning power. Whether they be Euclidean or Riemannian geometries, Boolean or Diophantine algebrae, reasoning power alone has constructed every known deductive system. Accordingly, the belief that the universe is structured like a superior deductive system entails a superior reasoning power. The belief in a superior reasoning power therefore seems as valid as the belief in the watch-maker by someone who had never seen a watch before.

Eirat

Yes, but there is still a difference between the two cases. In the case of the watch-finder, he could easily envisage a way of verifying that the watch was, in fact, man-made. He could travel the world over interrogating and observing until he found out whether or not the watch was indeed man-made. The physicist-theologian

44

can envisage no such verification technique. Therefore his affirmation of the existence of a superior reasoning power is meaningless, since it cannot be verified.

Dymon

If you mean that you do not accept as meaningful any empirical proposition which cannot be verified in the manner you suggest than I quite agree with you that the two cases are different. But I'd like you to note that we have not stated a metaphysical proposition. Our physicist-theologian has simply said, "The universe evidences a superior reasoning power." He has not said that this power exists now, or that it must have existed at one time, or that it acts in any particular manner. He has stated no proposition *about* it. He has, to put it in logical language, stated only that 'p' implies 'q'—that the belief common to all science that the universe reveals itself as analogous to a deductive system *implies* a superior reasoning power since a deductive system cannot exist apart from a reasoning power.

Eirat

Are you saying that all scientists believe in this superior reasoning power?

Dymon

No, I am saying only that they all *act* as if they do. Just imagine our space visitor again for a moment, if you will. Suppose that he were to tour some of our great research centers and institutions of learning and that he asked what the people were doing. Would you not be obliged to answer that insofar as their theoretical work were concerned they were doing one of two things. Either they were trying to elicit additional information concerning the phenomena in which they were interested, or they were trying to encompass a greater range of phenomena under a smaller but broader group of principles. Suppose that our visitor this time had not a wide scientific training but knew something of mathematics. He might say, "Whatever makes them think they can encompass a broader range of phenomena under a smaller number of wider principles?"

"Well," you might answer, "experience has taught them that nature is uniform so they believe that this uniformity will continue —that eventually we shall be able to describe all of nature from a small number of postulates [30] deriving, as it were from a deductive system, all of the detailed principles from the more broad."

[30] Such as Russell's five postulates of non-demonstrative inference.

45

Our visitor might well say, "What a remarkable religion they must have—what do they call it—science worship? They all seem to believe in a superior reasoning power manifesting itself in the universe."

Eirat

And should this superior reasoning power be called God?

Dymon

Call it what you like—God will do as well as any other name.

Eirat

But are you not overlooking the fact that the truth or falsity of a mathematical proposition is not dependent upon its ability to be derived as part of a deductive system? It is just as true standing on its own as it is when shown to be part of a deductive system. The Egyptians, for example, used the Pythagorean theorem for surveying land long before Pythagoras recognized its general validity. Then when its general validity was recognized, its truth was not dependent upon its derivation in a deductive system. It would seem therefore, that the propositions of physics, expressed in mathematical language, express empirical truths in no way dependent upon their being part of a deductive system.

Dymon

The answer to that is surely that to some people, the expression of one or more unrelated propositions of physics in mathematical language might evidence a superior reasoning power in the universe. To them the case is strengthened if the propositions form an almost complete deductive system.

Eirat

You would never obtain the assent of a conventional theologian to the view you are expressing. Theologians and metaphysicians seem to maintain, when they attempt to prove the existence of God, that their proof is demonstrably certain. You are suggesting that the evidence is non-demonstrative. Whereas they say the proof is like one of mathematics, you say it is like one of science or common sense.

Dymon

Well, we have seen, have we not, that the only statements which are demonstrably certain are those which are implicit in their own premises. As you are aware, these include propositions of logic as well as those of mathematics. The only reason they are invariably certain is that we do not allow them to be false. If someone dis-

46

puted the truth of a syllogism of Aristotelian logic, we would say he was mistaken as to the premises—if someone said 2 plus 2 is not equal to 4, we would say he had counted incorrectly. If finite addition be simply the memorized result of counting, we have really learned nothing when we learn to add, that was not already there when we learned to count. A demonstrative proof of the existence of God is a logical impossibility since we could not derive God as a conclusion from anything but demonstratively certain premises. Such an alleged proof could tell us nothing. The conclusion would be a tautology because the premises were tautologies.

Eirat

What you say is true about a demonstrative proof, but with respect to your non-demonstrative proof, may I remind you of what Ayer said:

"It is sometimes claimed, indeed, that the existence of a certain sort of regularity in nature constitutes sufficient evidence for the existence of a god. But, if the sentence 'God exists' entails no more than that certain types of phenomena occur in certain sequences, then to assert the existence of a god will be simply equivalent to asserting that there is the requisite regularity of nature; and no religious man would admit that this was all he intended to assert in asserting the existence of a god." [31]

Dymon

But we have noted that science goes a great deal farther than Ayer's example. It is not simply the case that science is concerned only with certain types of phenomena occurring in certain sequences. Ayer, in the quotation you mention, seems to me to be limiting the logic of science to an analysis of causation. If science were limited as he suggests to discovering sequences of phenomena, there would be no place for a Newton or an Einstein. Theoretical scientists go much farther. They concern themselves with the development of a deductive system which when applied to nature shall encompass all natural phenomena. This, in my submission, is a horse of another hue from Ayer's statement. I say again that if the scientist believes nature to be structured as a superior deductive system; and all his conduct indicates that he so believes, then he should believe also in a superior reasoning power for there has never been a deductive system apart from one derived from reasoning power.

[31] *Language, Truth & Logic,* page 115.

Eirat

I'm not sure I agree with you. Assuming that the scientist does believe the universe to be structured like a superior deductive system, has the system not, insofar as it is developed at present, been developed by the mind of man?

Dymon

Certainly it has—it has been a process of trial and error. Newton, for example, described the phenomenon of gravitation by a simple equation relating it with the mass of two bodies and the square of the distance between them. Einstein used general field equations describing gravitation as a property of space. Certainly the deductive system which fits in either case has been derived from the mind of man, but in their turn they have been implicit in nature. The mind of man *tries* the alternative deductive systems but it is *nature* which seems to be fitted with them. It is *nature* which manifests the deductive system. The mind of man merely tries to understand it.

Eirat

Let us not travel so quickly! There are certain preliminary questions we should examine here. When we say that nature manifests a deductive system, what are we really saying? Are we not simply substituting the language of quantity for the language of quality? Among natural phenomena which are measurable, some are apparently measurable in different manner than others. It is true that one measures any quantity by means of a length or an angle, and to that extent, all measurements of capacity, for example of length, area and volume, are apparently different from measurements of intensity, for example of electric potential and temperature. In the case of the former, we can fairly add the sum of two quantities, in the latter we cannot. It is correct to say for example that two yards are always twice one yard but whether or not a temperature is twice another depends upon the process used to measure temperature. As de Broglie has pointed out:

"We could nevertheless very well measure lengths with rulers graduated logarithmically like slide rules and then a length of two metres would not be double the measure of one metre." [32]

Similarly, measurements of intensity, for example temperature, can be expressed by defining the temperature of a body as proportional

[32] *Physics and Microphysics,* Louis de Broglie, page 81. See de Broglie for a detailed discussion of most of the matters mentioned on this page.

to the mean thermal energy of its molecules. This reconciles the idea of temperature to that of an entity which can be measured like length. (A perfect gas of N molecules is said to have a termperature double that of another perfect gas of N molecules if the energy of thermal agitation of the first gas is double that of the second). The difference between measuring factors of capacity and factors of intensity is therefore more apparent than real. There are, of course, different characteristics of the various quantities measured by science. There are the so-called scalar or invariant quantities, namely, those like temperature and electric charge which, as their name "scalar" suggests, can be represented by a scale of units independently of a reference in three dimensional space. Then there are quantities dependent upon a dimensional framework such as the vector of a point or the tensor of a phenomenon of higher order. The vectors and tensors of space-time have a significance independent of the observer, but their components, being the quantities which are observed and measured, differ according to the systems of reference of their observers. So the groundwork of science is simply measurement. To quote de Broglie again:

"Not being able at each instant to represent in its entirety the infinitely complex state of the real world of which, moreover, each observer at every instant perceives but a minute part, physics had sought to discover in the uninterrupted flux of phenomena certain elements capable at the time, of being detached from the totality by theoretical abstraction and of being characterized by precise numerical values. These elements are the 'observable physical quantities' and the aim of physical science is to establish the relations which exist between the values of these quantities and their variations, then to interpret these relations, to show their scope, by co-ordinating them in those vast constructions of the mind, which are called theories." [33]

So when we say that nature manifests the attributes of a deductive system, are we not saying only that physical phenomena characterized by numerical values are related to each other in the manner prescribed by the various deductive systems of mathematics? The deductive systems are "constructions of the mind" to be sure, but how else could these numerical values, since they are numerical, be related?

Dymon

That is precisely the point. Since they are numbers, any relation between them must be deductive.

[33] *Physics and Microphysics,* Louis de Broglie, page 78.

Eirat

But what, after all, is the significance of that? Listen to what Eddington says:

"Mind filters out matter from the meaningless jumble of qualities, as the prism filters out the colors of the rainbow from the chaotic pulsations of white light. Mind exalts the permanent and ignores the transitory; and it appears from the mathematical study of relations that the only way in which mind can achieve her object is by picking out one particular quality as the permanent substance of the perceptual world, partitioning a perceptual time and space for it to be permanent in, and, as a necessary consequence of this Hobson's choice, the laws of gravitation and mechanics and geometry have to be obeyed. Is it too much to say that mind's search for permanence has created the world of physics? The laws of electro-dynamics appear in like manner to depend merely on the identification of another permanent thing—electric charge. The conclusion is that the whole of those laws of nature which have been woven into a unified scheme—mechanics, gravitaton, electro-dynamics and optics—have their origin, not in any special mechanism of nature, but in the workings of the mind.
'Give me matter and motion,' said Descartes, 'and I will construct the universe.' The mind reverses this. 'Give me a world—a world in which there are relations—and I will construct matter and motion.'
We have found that where science has progressed the farthest, the mind has but regained from nature that which the mind has put into nature.
We have found a strange footprint on the shores of the unknown. We have devised profound theories, one after another, to account for its origin. At last, we have succeeded in reconstructing the creature that made the footprint. And lo! It is our own!" [34]

Dymon

Certainly a more eloquent spokesman than Eddington for this point of view would be difficult to find, but are the footprints entirely our own? Eddington says that by singling out matter as our primary quality, we have stacked the deck; that of necessity the laws of mechanics, gravitation and geometry follow. Also, that by singling out electric charge as another primary quality, that electrodynamics and optics follow. This is true, so that in one sense we *have* stacked the deck. But the interesting thing is that mechanics, gravitation, and geometry follow in the *manner* that they do—a manner, the numerical values of which, were not entirely fixed by us but certainly in some degree were fixed by nature.

[34] *Space, Time and Gravitation.*

Suppose we singled out instead of the static qualities, the dynamic ones as fundamental, we could still build a calculus of physics. It has been suggested that given a different intellectual structure from that of the mind of man, we could build a radically different physics. I'm not sure I can envisage a different intellectual structure, but assuming that I can, such intellect would develop a calculus of physics with which to structure nature.

The point is, however, that whatever deductive structures our minds can create for nature, they would be related to one another by some transformation system, some Rosetta stone. Thus nature itself has the attribute that it can be structured in only certain related ways.

Eirat

I expect your next step will be to tell me that since nature can only be so structured, that this evidences a superior reasoning power in nature itself, apart from the human mind which creates the structure. If so, I don't agree with you. Fabricating a physical structure for nature is really only a sophisticated version of what you do when you examine something with your eyes. When you look at something with your eyes there is a one-to-one correspondence between the points of the object in nature and the points in your brain created by the image on the retina. What difference in principle is there between the process of vision and the process of creating a physical structure? Both are products of the mind.

Dymon

Yes, but both tell us something about nature too. I agree with you that the manner in which information about nature appears to us, and indeed the fact that we can perceive anything at all, is dependent upon the structure of the mind and senses. For example, if we temporarily had eyes like a bighorn sheep it would appear to us equivalent to viewing the world with the acuity of eight-power binoculars.[35] Similarly, we could conceivably structure nature with a different type of physics. But the fact remains that whatever qualities we chose as primary in nature, certain numerical relationships between them would be fixed not by the mind but by nature. To use a concrete example, the mind has singled out mass as a quality which our universe possesses but the numerical ratio of the protons' and electrons' rest masses has been fixed not by the mind but by nature. In a similar way, my eye sees my window at approx-

[35] *Big Game Animals of North America,* Jack O'Connor

imately twice the distance that my desk is from the same eye. The relation is fixed not by my mind but by nature. To be sure, the perception of the relations and the symbols I use for their description are concepts of the mind, but the relations of which they are abstractions are nature's. To that extent the footprints are not our own. The word "footprint" and the image on the retina are ours, but the indentation on the shore is very often nature's. If I say, therefore, that the universe is structured like a superior deductive system and that accordingly it evidences a superior reasoning power, my statement seems valid, for while the human mind fashions the deductive structure it is nature which wears it. Nature, it is true, is indifferent to the qualities singled out for basing the structure but it is not indifferent to the numerical values contained in it. And it is the numerical values which give the structure its deductive character. The qualities to which we assign numerical values are the only things which distinguish physical propositions from exercises in pure mathematics.

Eirat

Eddington would not agree with you. He says:

"This is how our theory now stands. We have a world of point-events with their primary interval-relations. Out of these an unlimited number of more complicated relations and qualities can be built up mathematically, describing various features of the state of the world. These exist in nature in the same sense as an unlimited number of walks exist on an open moor. But the existence is, as it were, latent unless someone gives a significance to the walk by following it; and in the same way the existence of any one of these qualities of the world only acquires significance above its fellows, if a mind singles it out for recognition." [36]

Dymon

If this contradicts what I've been saying, I can only plead that I do not agree with Eddington. He says that relations can be built up mathematically describing various features of the state of the world. But it is the numerical values which distinguish these features. The analogy of an unlimited number of walks on an open moor seems accurate if restricted to the choice of qualities but is hardly accurate in treating the features of the physical worlds which follow when once the choice of primary qualities has been made. The number of walks are not then unlimited. They are to a large extent prescribed by nature. The mathematical relations are

[36] *Space, Time and Gravitation.*

fixed as is the course of a traveller, not on an open moor but on a plain with high hills scattered thereon. It seems to me that nature, in fixing certain mathematical relations between whatever qualities we choose for her description, evidences a deductive character synonymous with reasoning power. It therefore seems to me an empirical statement to say that nature evidences a superior reasoning power.

Eirat

I cannot agree that nature evidences a superior reasoning power. Your argument it seems to me is based upon poor semantics. But even assuming that you are right and assuming further that this superior reasoning power is called "God", of what use is the concept? You have said yourself that it is nonsense to speak of God as a creator in space-time—you say that to propound two sets of laws in the universe, one physical, the other divine, is likewise nonsense —you say that the idea of a life hereafter betrays an inadequate knowledge of biology—of what use then is the concept God? Are we, who are also governed by physical laws, part of the great deductive system?

Dymon

It would appear that we are. We are, in the classical theologian's view, an equation in God's deductive system—a note in His symphony—a thought in His mind. Is it any wonder that the religious man says, "God is in me and I am in God"?

Eirat

The moment you depart from using language in its verifiable sense you are talking nonsense. Who can verify and how can he verify that God is *in* anyone?

Dymon

Am I? As Russell says, is the proposition "All of the numbers which will not be thought of before the year 2000 are greater than 1,000," a nonsensical one? Yet it cannot be verified. Is a symphony nonsense? A symphony cannot be verified and yet it can be said to be *in* its composer.

Eirat

A symphony uses sounds but it doesn't *purport* to use language or to express a proposition which can be verified.

Dymon

Neither does the man who uses the word God. He is not saying, "Mr. Smith, I'd like you to shake the hand of God."

Eirat

But he is using *words* and if he intends to express anything he must use them in the verifiable sense.

Dymon

Why should he use words only in the verifiable sense? It is important, I agree, to distinguish the different ways in which a proposition can be true, but is our criterion of meaning so rigorous that it must exclude statements like "God is in me and I am in God"? The person who hears such a statement knows very well that his informant is not saying that God is a physiological organ situate between the liver and the spleen. If you rule out religious statements as meaningless, you'll have to do the same with certain psychological ones. When Freud spoke of the ego and super-ego he knew that one wouldn't find their physical equivalent in an autopsy. He created the concepts to give meaning to otherwise unrelated psychological phenomena. He said that the mind acts *as if* there were a trap door between the conscious and the unconscious —*as if* there were an ego and super-ego. Do the behaviorist psychologists not lose a valuable tool when they refuse to recognize psychological entities? Do the rest of us not lose a valuable tool if we exclude all religious statements as intellectually meaningless?

Eirat

That's substantially the question I asked a moment ago. Of what use is the concept God? If you can show me a *use* for it I'll accept it as meaningful.

Dymon

Well, if God means a superior reasoning power as I have said it does then the universe is no longer the same place it was before we recognized that fact. One feels an integral part of it—not an unexplained accident. It would appear also that the concept of God as a superior *reasoning* power is significant.

It is one thing to envisage a superior *power* in the universe—in which case one thinks of something like Newtonian gravitation or electromagnetism. It is quite another to envisage a superior *reasoning* power. In the latter case a *person* is called to mind because we associate reasoning power with a mind.

Eirat

Aren't you getting close to the theory of the old man sitting on a cloud?

Dymon

I don't think so. I have justification for assuming reasoning power but no body. True, no one has ever seen a mind apart from a body, nevertheless our belief in a superior deductive system evidences only reasoning power, not muscle and bone. Hence, I say that the idea of a *personal* God is not without meaning.

Eirat

I have already said that it seems to me you are falling into error, but I'll refrain from interrupting your exposition. What other conclusions can you draw from your superior reasoning power?

Dymon

Well, as I said before, although this concept of God is a personal one, there is no justification for assuming any manifestation of this God *outside* the laws of science. The whole superstitious apparatus of miracles and direct intervention is therefore gone.

Eirat

Your God is rather austere then?

Dymon

To some extent, yes. But surely the "death of God" theologians are right when they repeat what the philosophers have stated, that is, that we are better off without supernatural miracles and the primitive apparatus of a life hereafter including a heaven and a hell. Concepts such as these inhibit the mind and restrict the understanding.

Eirat

I agree with what you say with respect to the hereafter. I agree also that there is no justification for a belief in miracles and that such belief restricts the understanding, but I wonder if this restriction appears the same to you as it does to me.

Dymon

Well, take the most famous miracle of the Christian religion, for example, the belief that on the third day Christ arose from the dead. Is this not a superstitious belief? After all, what is the evidence? It has been argued before that this was a strong man in the prime of life who was crucified. And what is crucifixion? It consists of being nailed through the hands and feet to a cross and placed in an erect position for a few hours. The evidence indicates also a spear wound in the side. Is this sufficient to kill a man such as this? Ask yourself if a modern Court, presented with this evidence, and also with evidence that the man was taken down, placed in a cave and was seen by witnesses three days later to be up and about again, would a Court presume the death of the man for the purposes of probating his estate or compelling payment of his life insurance? The idea is preposterous. But what is more important, it is entirely unnecessary. Are the man's teachings less true for all of this? Is the sermon on the mount any the less remarkable? Is the whole story not ten times more beautiful when seen to be completely natural, completely free from supernatural miracles? This is what I mean by restricting the understanding.[37] The whole idea of two sets of laws, one physical, the other divine, is not only irrational, it is ugly. Further, it is unnecessary even to the religious person. We have seen that a belief in God as I have described it can only be empirical and thus not dependent upon such things as miracles. I do not intend here to embark upon a naturalistic interpretation of Scripture but I am, nonetheless, satisfied it can be done. I would go further. It seems to me that the development of a Christian ethic as set out in the sermon on the mount is so inseparably a part of human nature that given the existence of a primitive society in an isolated environment, a similar ethic would inevitably arise—as indeed it has in other religions.

Eirat

All you have mentioned so far is the existence of a rational, personal God. If this God is not manifest in the affairs of men except through the medium of scientific laws, of what use is he?

Dymon

You have stated a use yourself. The concept of the creation of man by God, for example, is a sensible one if creation means the development of organic life from the inorganic and the evolution of man from primitive organic species. Does it not make sense to say that this is God manifesting himself in accordance with scientific laws?

Eirat

It may make sense but it certainly doesn't *add* anything. I expect you will also tell me that if the accounts of heredity are examined there is a basis for a kind of biological immortality. But what psychological difference does your account of God make? After all, you've shown no *physical* difference.

Dymon

Yes, that's the most important thing to the religious man—the

[37] A theologian who recently read this account of the resurrection criticized it on the ground that the argument had been first advanced early in this century and was therefore "old hat". It seems to me it is older hat than that. It may also have been advanced by Doubting Thomas.

psychological aspect. If there is a basis for a personal, rational God, there is a basis also for man saying, "God is in me and I am in God."

Eirat

How so? What is such a man saying?

Dymon

It's not so much a question of what he's saying—it's what he's *feeling*. The statement tells us that he believes this superior power to be manifest in himself and that introspectively, he feels himself to be a part of the superior power. Is there anything wrong with that? It's a question of attitude, feeling and psychological conviction based not upon any particular intellectual premise but upon the whole of the individual's attitude, knowledge and experience. There is no point in asking such a man to verify what he says. He's already verified it by his own introspective psychological standards or he wouldn't say it. Similarly, you will not convince such a person that he is making a meaningless or tautological statement. It has tremendous significance to him. It connects him, the observer, with what he observes—so that he feels part of it.

Eirat

But you chose a moment ago the analogy of a man saying, "I've got a symphony in me." Let us take the simpler case of a man who says, "There's a song in my heart." This is not a meaningless or tautological statement. It can even be verified. When he says it, you believe that he is happy, that he might dance or sing at any moment, or that he may sit down and write a song. You know he's telling you something about his psychological state.

Dymon

Well, is not the statement, "God is in me and I am in God" analogous in some respects? Wouldn't you expect such a man to act a little differently from one who would not say such a thing? You wouldn't be surprised if he knelt in prayer or did good works, but more important, you have learned something about his psychological state.

Eirat

But the man who says, "There's a song in my heart" really has a song in his heart, unless of course he's lying.

Dymon

Are you suggesting that the man who says, "God is in me"

57

really hasn't got God in him? Has he not the superior reasoning power in him to some extent?

Eirat

I see the analogy. I hope you see the difference. What puzzles me, however, is why men strive to rationalize a deity. You, for example, have obviously devoted some time to thought of these matters—why? Is it a question of the religious dialogue?

Dymon

Religious dialogue?

Eirat

Yes. Is prayer not the most significant concomitant of religion? I've often wondered if it isn't the root of the religious impulse in man. Prayer is a dialogue between man and God. Therefore, the search for God is a defense mechanism for the man who feels he may after all be talking to himself.

Dymon

No, I think the religious impulse is more fundamental than the religious dialogue. It doesn't appear to me to be dependent upon the development of language. It probably existed before language did. I can quite well imagine a savage who, reared in isolation, had never learned a language and who could not communicate with his kind, yet who manifested all the characteristics of a mystic. There would be no question for him of the "religious dialogue." Prayer would be meaningless to him. Yet he would have no inhibitions about his reverence. The feeling might well be powerful enough to compel him to sit with rapt and open heart in contemplation of the boundless world around him—this without a single word in his vocabulary with which to express the communion he felt with "the infinite".

Eirat

What do you mean by communion with the infinite? Is the infinite a mathematical expression? If so, we are immediately involved in the various orders of infinity—for example, the infinity of all integers and fractions as compared to the infinity of all geometrical curves. They are not even of the same order of infinity. The latter is larger, although both are infinite. I take it that the infinity of which you speak is not the same as the mathematical concept. Indeed, it could not be because your savage cannot use language, let alone mathematical language.

Dymon

It is difficult to try to describe "communion with the infinite". The phrase itself is not very helpful because it describes a psychological state or attitude in no way dependent upon the logical processes we associate with language. In the civilized world, however, we are so accustomed to the use of language that there is a barrier raised by language itself. This barrier must be surmounted before a "communion with the infinite" can be experienced, for indeed, it is not a question of understanding but of experiencing it. The barrier is this—one must believe in "the infinite" or "God" as a necessary pre-condition to such experience. It may sound paradoxical that on the one hand an inarticulate savage could experience such communion while on the other hand articulate, modern man could not, unless first he believed in "the infinite" or "God", but on closer examination the paradox disappears. The savage is doing something without the necessity of explaining, even to himself, what he's doing, while modern man, more conscious of himself, requires the concept to be explained to his intellectual satisfaction.

Eirat

You are using the words "infinite" and "God" interchangeably.

Dymon

Indeed I am. We have seen that our use of "infinite" is not the mathematical usage. Yet it is in some respects more palatable than the word "God". But you can substitute the word "God" for "the infinite" in "communion with the infinite". What I said still holds —unlike the inarticulate savage, modern man must intellectually rationalize "the infinite" or "God" before the communion can occur. Just in passing, we should note that there is a difference between the expressions "God" and "the infinite"—they are not completely interchangeable. "God" is a more personalized expression and lends itself to development, as you say, of the religious dialogue, namely prayer. "The infinite" would find more favor with a pure mystic like a Yogi. The reason for this is that to the Yogi "the infinite" is more a psychological force and less personified than is "God" to the western believer. Basic to both, however, is a state of mind analogous to "belief" as used in a proposition like "I believe such and such to be the case." In fact, if it were possible to say "I believe," without saying what it was that one believed, indeed, without having anything in mind which one *did* believe, the requisite state of mind would be present for "communion with the infinite" for it is after all a psychological state or attitude, not a factual belief.

Eirat

The power of positive thinking?

Dymon

Yes, you might say that. But as I have tried, clumsily perhaps, to explain—for modern man to achieve the same communion as the inarticulate savage, he must first *believe*. The belief orients modern man psychologically to the same attitude that the naive savage achieves naturally. Hence modern man's concern for a rational foundation for his religious impulse. If one believes that nature manifests a superior reasoning power, the groundwork had been laid for "communion with the infinite" and one may without intellectual embarrassment participate in the religious experience.

Eirat

Well, it has certainly taken you a long time to reach this conclusion. But I must say I remain unconvinced. I am certainly not free of the intellectual embarrassment you speak of. Assume that we are in possession of assumptions of physics from which all physical phenomena are explicable as theorems. What then? I agree with you that such deductive system would be a product of mind. But suppose that the numerical relations of this system were other than what they are or suppose that all physical processes controlled by the 2nd law of thermodynamics operated in reverse. Would these states of affairs not also be capable of description by deductive systems similar to the one we have assumed? Would they not equally be products of the mind? And on your reasoning would they not also be evidence of the superior reasoning power you speak of? I see nothing significant in the universe being *as it is* and thus the deductive system being as it is. In your criticism of Eddington, you said that the universe itself imposes certain of the properties of the deductive system used to describe it, but this is no different from a landscape imposing upon a painter the colors he must use to describe it (if he wishes to be photographic). Nor is there, I submit, a religious significance to the development of *any* physical deductive system. So long as physical relationships of any kind can be observed they can be described mathematically. To fail to recognize this is to fail to recognize that mathematical propositions are linguistic conventions similar to the propositions of ordinary language. When I say, for example, "This is black," there are implicit in my statement a number of other propositions, namely, that "it is not pink, not yellow, not white." Now you might say that these latter propositions follow deductively from the first just as certain theorems follow in a deductive system. But you would *not* say that because of the deductive character of the relations between these propositions that they evidence a superior reasoning power. No, you apparently say that only when a *mathematical* deductive system is found to fit. You say it when your pure mathematics has become applied. Why do you not say, for example, that our capacity to describe the colors of the spectrum of light evidences a superior reasoning power in nature? After all, if you're going to make this statement when you're assigned a number to these colors, that is to say, when you've allotted a frequency or wave length to them, then why not say it when you're still using "pink" and "red" and "green"?

I think that if you reflect for a moment upon what you have stated yourself about the inarticulate savage you might agree with me. You stated on the one hand that the unself conscious savage might "commune with the infinite" even though he had no language and a fortiori no mathematics. This indicates to me *not* the necessity for an intellectual rationale of religion in modern man but the fallacious character of any intellectual rationale so derived. You are quite right, I think, in suggesting that language, and in particular, scientific language, created the barrier between man and his religious impulse, but I think you are wrong in suggesting that a belief in a superior reasoning power is a necessary pre-condition for the exercise of such impulse.

In my view, after you have laboriously developed your intellectual justification for "the superior reasoning power", as you have done, you should see not only that it is fallacious but that it is completely unnecessary. You stated yourself that your "communion with the infinite" was not an intellectual belief but was analogous to the state of mind which exists when one says, "I believe," without having anything particular in mind which one does believe. So be it—why try to create an intellectual structure as a crutch for such psychological state? If that state is present you may participate in the "religious dialogue" or "communion with the infinite", for if when you've climbed the ladder you find that it is, after all, a faulty ladder, what need is there to repair it? You don't need a ladder. You're already there. You will not fall without the ladder. Your humanity will hold you up, as I hope to show you. The argument as you put it is really little more than a variant of the classical "argument from design". You will remember William James' statement,

"The argument from design reasons, from the fact that nature's laws are mathematical, and her parts benevolently adapted to each other, that this cause is both intellectual and benevolent." [38]

There is, I think, a similarity between your "superior reasoning power" and the argument from design.

You will perhaps agree that my criticisms of "beginning" and "creation of something out of nothing" demolish the cosmological argument. This argument, as you know, reasons from the existence of the universe to a first cause. Therefore, if you admit also my criticism of your "superior reasoning power" then nothing remains of the classical theological arguments, except possibly the argument "ex consensu gentium". As you know, this argument reasons that the belief in God is so widespread as to be grounded in the rational nature of man, and should therefore carry authority with it. I intimated earlier that this, in my opinion, is no argument at all. I am inclined now to think I may have been too peremptory.

If you must have an argument, this may be the only one you *can* have, for consider how widespread the religious experience really is. And before we go much farther let me say that by "religious experience" I mean, as you did, the psychological state which exists in the religious person when he says "God is in me and I am in God." You have noted the similarity between such a statement and that of the person who says, "There's a song in my heart." It is perhaps possible that the argument "ex consensu gentium" has seemed invalid not because it really is invalid but because of a mistaken idea of the character of certain religious statements. We have seen that physical propositions are little different from any other statements of fact. They merely substitute quantitative concepts for qualitative ones. But they do have in common with other factual propositions that they can be verified. A statement about length, temperature or electricity is true or false as it can be verified. "This room is 12 feet wide," or "This circuit is carrying 110

[38] *The Varieties of Religious Experience,* William James, page 428.

volts," entail techniques of measurement and comparison for their verification. The physicist is saying of the room, for example. "First you get a stick and take it to the Bureau of Standards where you trim it to the exact length of another stick called a foot. Then you place the stick down at one end of the room and turn it end over end along the wall until you reach the other side of the room. If you drop a marble in a jar for each side of the stick which is up as you do this, you'll have twelve marbles in the jar when you're finished. The twelve is, of course, simply a concept called number which applies to a set of classes when you make a side by side correspondence between each of the members of one class in the set and the members of any other class in the set. Any other room which is 12 feet wide is, of course, one which yields the same number of marbles, using the same stick."

Now, this technique does not, after all, differ materially from that of a mystic explaining "communion with the infinite". He might say, "First you sit in a quiet location in a comfortable position. You then expel from your mind all thought of mundane matters, close your eyes, and concentrate your attention on a point midway along the top of your scalp. Now open your heart like a tap and allow yourself to become a part of your environment. Soon you will experience a renewed emotional vigor, as one does when in love. This is 'communion with the infinite'."

This account appears equally as empirical as that of the stick and the marbles. Does it not possess the same inductive character? The mystic is saying that if you do this, you will find such and so to be the case. What is wrong with saying, "That which the mystic feels communion *with* is God"?

Dymon

There is perhaps this difference. The man with the stick and the marbles is convinced that anyone else using the same technique as he *must,* if he does it correctly, arrive at the same result. The experience of the mystic on the other hand is personal.

Eirat

I am suggesting now that the mystic is of the same opinion as to the universality of his technique. Perhaps a blind man could not carry out the stick and marble technique because of his physical impairment. The mystic says that anyone who is not emotionally impaired can carry out his technique. He has confidence that the normal man will duplicate his feat just as the physicist has confi-

63

dence that his can be duplicated. Hence I say that the argument "ex consensu gentium", if you need an argument, is perhaps the clincher. The religious impulse is probably latent or active in all men, and if it is, then the argument to support it is similar to the statistical arguments of nuclear physics. As you know, these arguments do not purport to describe with certainty the position and speed of, for example, an orbiting electron, but merely give the statistical probability of these values. The argument, ex consensu gentium, is similar in character despite the fact that a mathematical probability cannot be assigned to it. Lacking a statistical analysis we must investigate the impulse where we find it. We must ask the religious man what "God" means to him.

Dymon

He might simply reply, "God is pure nothing," or perhaps, "God is love." These are two of the conventional answers.

Eirat

Precisely! And it is no mere coincidence that he says this, for when he has practiced the mystical technique or undergone any other religious experience, he has found that God *is* "love" or *is* "pure nothing". You have said yourself that this is not a matter of a conviction based upon the expression of an attitude or psychological state. So it boils down to this that the religious man, at least by our definition, is one who *experiences* these feelings. Perhaps I can do no better than to quote Wittgenstein:

"The meaning of the word is the use we make of it." [39]

If such be the case, the meaning of the word "God", like the meaning of the word "electron" is the use we make of it. If we use it, it has meaning. If we do not, it has not. The religious man frequently uses the word "God". It so happens that in his meditations he often experiences a kind of abstract love. There is no other word for it—that is how it strikes him. In those meditations, he is unable to divorce his "love" from a quasi-human character. I suppose this is natural, since we most often associate love with human beings. Therefore, to him it becomes personified. The personification he calls "God". Psychology has never come close to explaining satisfactorily why this is so. But then why should we *expect* psychology adequately to explain the religious aspects of the human psyche? The human psyche must be at least as complex as

[39] My notes of Wittgenstein's lectures at Cambridge University contain this expression.

the human body is. Yet no one professes an ability to describe adequately the human body. Such explanations as there are pass through biology and microbiology to some enormously difficult problems. Why should anyone think that the human psyche is any less complex? Surely it must have evolved, layer upon layer, strand by strand with the concomitant biological processes of the body. All we know for sure is what we observe. We observe the religious impulse; we must therefore accept it as fact.[40] The religious man simply accepts the religious impulse as part of his humanity, and since he finds the impulse in himself, he assumes that it is likewise in others. If my observation of others is accurate, then he is correct. For "God" in the sense of "love" is in them, too—and it is often greatest in those who deny it most.

Dymon

Then are you not approaching the view of those theologians who say that a belief in God is a matter of faith rather than of reason?

Eirat

I thought you'd get around to that. And the answer is "no". This theological view assumes that there are two ways of believing something. One is on the basis of evidence and the other, that of faith, is on the basis of revelation or intuition, or is simply authoritatively accepted. The latter method of belief, that of faith, really should not be called belief at all unless it too satisfies our ordinary criteria for "belief".

Dymon

You admit, however, that there is this dichotomy.

Eirat

I hope to persuade you that the dichotomy is more apparent than real, and to do so I say this: The religious man *believes,* without necessarily believing *in* anything; the religious man *is in love,* without necessarily being in love *with* anything; the religious man *trusts,* without necessarily trusting *in* anything. That is why you will never shake the "conviction" of the truly religious man—for on the one hand there is nothing there to shake while on the other, you would have to shake human nature itself.

Dymon

To you, then, the "religious man" is simply "man".

---

[40] Jung appears to be one of the few who has accepted this fact and given it weight in his description of the human psyche.

Eirat

Certainly! Man's religious nature, in the sense I describe, is as much a part of his psyche as the fact that he is biped is part of his physiognomy.

Dymon

Let me be certain I understand you. From your criticism of my "argument from design", as you call it; from your appeal to the ubiquitous character of religious experience, that is to say, the argument "ex consensu gentium"; and from your conclusion that the religious impulse is not based upon evidence of external nature, are you saying it follows that religious love, if I may so use the expression, is a part of man's psychological make-up in the same way that conjugal love is?

Eirat

Indeed I am! The analogy is not without merit. If you were to read any of the books on functional psychology, you would find experimenters observing and classifying patterns of behaviour in terms of "instincts", "innate impulses", and conflicts of "id", "ego" and "super-ego". Such writers attempt to explain human behaviour in functional terms. But what they are really doing is attempting to classify this behaviour in accordance with certain abstract common denominators. These denominators are their starting points, just as the concept "number" is a starting point for much of mathematics. Take, for example, the "instinct of self-preservation" or the "reproductive instinct"—these are simply labels used to explain the contents of the bottle. If you asked a functional psychologist to explain to you the instinct of self-preservation, he would cite to you instances common to all species, of creatures protecting their lives. When he was finished you might say, "Oh, you mean that this instinct is the name you give to the *probability* that the creature will react in such and such a way." Well, in greater or less degree is the religious impulse not somewhat analogous? True, it does not appear evident in the lower mammals—you've undoubtedly never seen a camel praying—but you have observed such behaviour in man. We have probably both seen men in situations of great stress, men who had perhaps never in their lives before exhibited any religious behaviour, and we have watched them behave in a religious manner. I have seen it so frequently and in such marked degree that I cannot do otherwise than conclude that it was part of their humanity and in this regard, it matters not whether you use functional terms like "instincts" or behaviourable language. The phenomenon or behaviour is there to be observed.

Dymon

Yes, but I have seen such people immediately afterwards repudiate this behaviour too. They would not admit it even to themselves.

Eirat

Surely that may be the result of either of two things. Either they are poor observers of their own behaviour or being possessed of preconceived positions on the question of religion they interpret their reactions as weakness or as being intellectually unsound.

There are, of course, people who may genuinely never experience a religious impulse. I think it not unlikely that some people are incapable of it. They may be emotionally impaired—just as the psychologists tell us that some persons are incapable of conjugal love. I think too, that in a closely knit society, people may perhaps be less prone to the religious experience, but show me a thoughtful man who has lived much of his life in solitude and danger and I will show you a religious man. Perhaps there is here a clue to the religious aspect of man's psyche—certainly throughout all but the most recent part of his biological evolution man has been subjected individually to greater physical danger and to more solitude than he is today. I think that if, as Aristotle says, "Man is a political animal", he is undoubtedly also a religious animal.

Dymon

Wittgenstein said in his "Tractatus",

"Whereof one cannot speak, one must remain silent."

What you have said is like that. If I understand you correctly, the religious man may *feel,* but he may not *speak.* The moment he begins to speak, he is really doing nothing more than describing his own psychological state or his own feelings—feelings which, it is true, are undoubtedly shared by others—but which, like his aesthetic judgements, are reactions to his environment or to representations of his environment—like pictures.

Eirat

Your comparison with a work of art is not the best one. You have excluded music from aesthetics. Music would have, for your analogy, the advantage that it evokes feelings in the listener or the composer which are not necessarily based upon anything in nature. Even mathematics would have been a better analogy, for the mathematician may experience great intellectual delight from his work without *applying* his mathematics to anything in nature. If I have led you to believe that the religious man cannot speak, I apologize. I meant to convey that he should understand what it is he is speaking *about*.

Dymon

Well, what *is* he speaking about? Perhaps it is true that all he is doing is describing his own psychological state.

Eirat

I don't think so. The source material for his utterances is introspective, it is true, and accordingly he is frequently criticized as not being "objective", but that is not to say that he is merely describing his own psychological state.

Dymon

How so?

Eirat

Well, suppose that a man were to observe some of the more obvious facts of his own physiognomy. For example, that he had a truncated body and a head. And suppose further that he concluded from his self-observation that everyone had such a body and head. Would he, like the religious man, be criticized for not being objective—for not examining everyone in the world to see if his general proposition were inductively valid? Of course not! So long as he were careful not to conclude that everything he observed about himself was true of others, he would be safe from criticism. He might, for example, conclude that everyone had fair skin—in this self-observation he would be wrong. Therefore, the self-observation alone might be misleading if not verified against either his own observation of others or their observations of themselves. (I don't wish, in this latter connection, to become embroiled in argument about whether or nor what *he* observes is the same as that which someone else observes. He might say, "By fair skin, I mean this . . ." pointing to a shade on a color chart, ". . . and I assume that you see it in the same way I do.") The point is, he would not be criticized if he proceeded in the manner I have described for the same reason that a nuclear physicist is not criticized for not examining all of the uranium ($_{92}U^{235}$) nuclei in the world when he predicts the typical reaction of one such nucleus when hit by a neutron. The scientist has faith in the regularity of nature.[41] Well, the religious man has faith in the regularity of *human* nature. I think that the introspective observations of the religious man can be meaningful. His subject matter is different from that of the scientist—that's all.

Dymon

Are you now going to tell me that the nuclear physicist should forsake his cyclotron and bevatron and focus his attention instead on the top of his scalp?

Eirat

You know very well I am not. But I do say that the religious man, if he is careful, can make discoveries just as startling as those of the physicist.

Dymon

Then you must be suggesting, as William James did, that someone should study "religious experience"; that is to say, should classify and analyze the various types of religious experience, using as it were for his raw materials, all of the writings of the recognized saints and mystics.

Eirat

That may be a laudable objective, I don't know. But it is not what I am suggesting. Such a study might, I suspect, yield little but intellectual indigestion. No, the most obvious source material for the religious man is his own psyche. It is the traditional source material and really is the only one available. If he is careful, what he finds should be verified by others.

Dymon

Well, let's get on with it. What can he find? If my suspicions are correct, we are going to end up pretty close to poetry, after having first got all muddied up with functional psychology.

Eirat

No, I don't intend to discuss the religious impulse in the same way that the psychologist does—that is to say, by using it to explain human behaviour, but rather to discuss it as you would any other observed phenomenon. First of all, I think we must get clear that while the religious man *is* describing his own psyche, he is

[41] He has faith in something like Russell's five postulates of non-demonstrative inference.

69

saying something more. He is saying, "And what is more, I think I am describing something which is common to *all* men—that your psyche is basically the same as mine."

Dymon

I will go along with you that far. I think it makes sense for a man to say, "Biologically, you and I have evolved together; psychologically we have done the same."

Eirat

I don't profess to be able to trace this psychological evolution. Bold indeed would be he who did, but studies of simpler mammals and indeed of simpler peoples have begun to fill the gaps for the psychologist. We also have some substantial knowledge concerning the sensory mechanisms. Quite apart from how we got this way, we seem to have considerable knowledge of what we *are*. We suggested earlier that a person under stress reacts toward a deity. It has been said that he is regressing to an infantile state where he looked to a parent for protection, but this theory does nothing to explain the religious impulse in situations where there is no undue stress. For this we must look elsewhere. I think it amounts to this—biologically, man is in a constant state of greater or less anxiety. This anxiety, all other factors being equal, is perhaps greater, the sharper are his senses and his imagination. He must therefore establish an intellectual rapport with his environment— even if he stays strictly within his habitat in the ecological sense. To achieve such intellectual quiescence, man must recognize that evolutionary laws have operated upon him and have made him what he is *psychologically* as well as physiologically. Death, reproduction, natural selection, mutation and adaptation have operated just as surely to mould man's psyche as they have to sculpt his body. Introspective examination shows him that the personality bequeathed to him by his ancestors is indeed quite a remarkable one. Clearly it is disposed to believe, disposed to trust, and disposed to love. It will readily be agreed that without such personality, belief could not be confuted, trust could not be misplaced and love could not be unrequited. We must assume that such personality has been biologically useful to man. Without it man could not have *learned;* without the elements of it, he could not have *evolved.* Look now at *any* book on clinical psychology— whether it be based upon Freud, James, McDougall, Watson, Jung or Pavlov—you will find infants learning to crawl, going to the bathroom, and to the schoolroom. You will find a child growing up to be an immensely active, curious, sensitive human animal; you will see him learning and performing tasks of prodigious complexity. Could any "free association" or "conditioned response" possibly operate in such personality if it were not disposed to believe, to trust, to love? You may say that dogs possess rudiments of these traits (which I will call positive traits) as well as man, and you would be correct. But man alone appears to be *conscious* of them. Is it so remarkable then that man's consciousness of these traits should, when the focus of such traits is not directed upon any particular object or thing, appear to his intellect as "the infinite", to his emotion as "love" and to his conviction as "faith"? We should long ago have connected man's consciousness of these traits in the abstract with "God". God is what you believe in when your belief is pure belief—unfocussed. God is where your love is when your love is unspecified. God is that in which you trust when your trust is pure, and has thus been weaned from any particular trust. God is the affirmation of all that is best in man. God is the pure and abstract expression of the human personality.

Dymon

Hold on! I can see the abstract trait of "love", that is to say "love" divorced from any person or thing, since I can experience it, but I'm having difficulty with "the infinite".

Eirat

Yes, I did too at first. Now, I wonder why I didn't see it long ago. "The infinite" in the religious sense, as we noted earlier, has nothing to do with the concept of infinite space. Neither has it anything to do with mathematical infinity. It is a purely subjective concept. This, I think, is what the religious man means when he says that God (the infinite) is beyond space-time. He shouldn't have said it is *beyond* space-time, since it has *nothing to do with* space-time. "The infinite", as he uses it, is introspective—it is what he observes when he looks *within* himself, not something in the physical world. He practices a mystical discipline or undergoes a religious experience—and by this I mean nothing mysterious— he simply opens his heart and mind and *feels* something like love as a result. He observes that the abstract object of this feeling is not limited, or bounded in any way. It *is* infinite. What is more, he *believes* in the existence of the abstraction upon which his personality is focussed. Similarly, with regard to the concept "faith". We here have a man who has experienced this love not focussed upon

71

any particular object or thing. He has experienced it with both his heart and his mind. It appears to him that its object is infinite in dimension. Further, although he looked inward to see it, it appears to be an outward related experience. If he calls that which he has introspectively observed, "God", does it not follow that he is intellectually justified in having "faith"—in *believing* in "God"? After all, he has literally observed this phenomenon just as a scientist *observes* physical phenomena—and please don't inform me that a scientist *sees* a phenomenon with his eyes, whereas a religious man's observation is not with his eyes. The answer to that is that the scientist *sees* very little of the phenomenon he observes. The only real difference is that the religious man has no way of *measuring* what he observes. But surely he would not be acting rationally if he denied his own introspective observation. To the contrary, he usually relies upon this experience in times of anxiety or stress to cleanse his mind and his emotions, to give him the strength and courage he might not otherwise have. He makes this observation part of his daily life. What is more, he observes that others do the same thing. So he knows it is not something peculiar to himself alone. He knows it is part of his humanity. As I said, it appears to him that this abstraction is outside of, and apart from him—and it certainly is, if what he observes is the end product of a psychological evolution lasting some one billion years.

Dymon

The kingdom of God is within, is that it?

Eirat

It most definitely is!

Dymon

On your analysis, however, God simply arises in the individual man as an abstraction from examination of his own personality. How could God in such circumstances not be human—how could he be divine?

Eirat

How could he be anything else? The concept "divinity" usually means something apart from the world in which we live and this observed abstraction is not part of the workaday world. Isn't this the sort of thing people have in mind when they consider that Christ was divine? He represented the perfect abstraction of man. It was only when he became an abstraction that he became divine. There is, of course, another sense of "divinity", and that is the idea of omnipotence. But people who practice religious techniques are not behaving irrationally when they consider omnipotent this abstraction of the positive traits I have described. Faith can move mountains because first of all it can move *you*. And it can move you because this faith is not focussed upon any particular chimeral thing but arises from the general human personality and is focussed like a telescope upon an abstraction. It is founded upon bedrock because it is based in the human personality and its focus, since it is not specific, cannot shift.

Dymon

I follow you in part. And I think I can agree with you that man possesses a personality disposed to believe and to trust and to love. While this description is undoubtedly a psychological over-simplification, it appears that any intelligent theory of learning must start from some such premise. Indeed the human mind must of necessity first learn to believe and to trust and to love in simple material things and human relationships before these positive traits are sufficiently evident to be observed per se, but my mind balks at the definition of God as their abstract focal target. As you have seen, we have talked of specific, primitive gods, and later of my "superior reasoning power". But these were not abstractions in the sense you have described. When believed in they were *there*—outside of us so to speak—but nevertheless there.

Eirat

You remind me of a person who is examining a sunflower under an overcast sky. He might say, "It keeps turning, as if following a light." Such person, if he had lived his whole life under an overcast sky, would say, "There must be some mysterious object up there it focusses upon." So it is with the religious man whose personality is focussed upon the abstract object of these positive human traits. Is he not more apt to be correct than the person who says, "He's not focussed on anything." At least the religious man has observed the focal process. He is more correct than the one who would deny that it exists. If a particle of iron tends to be aligned in a magnetic field why can a human personality not be aligned and focussed in a particular manner?

Dymon

Ah, yes, but a magnetic field is only part of the general phenomenon of electromagnetism. Even if we cannot see a magnetic field we know it is there because, for one thing, we can change or vary it.

Eirat

I thought you'd say that. So let us look a little more closely at the concept "field". We speak of electric fields and magnetic fields. Even space-time is a kind of field. It is a geometric field which is utilized to describe the structure and motion of inertial mass. You will have noticed, however, that some fields can be varied while others cannot. We can vary certain small electric, magnetic or space-time fields by bringing to bear outside influences but we cannot, for example, appreciably vary the earth's magnetic field or the gravitational space-time field of the solar system. Let us then synthesize the concept "field" as applied for instance to the phenomenon of magnetism with its application to the phenomenon of the human personality.

Dymon

This should be interesting.

Eirat

I hope it will be. What if, for example, a particle of iron were endowed with consciousness of a kind where the particle knew that it was itself incapable of changing its spatial alignment. Now place it in a magnetic field. Would it not *observe* that it had become aligned or polarized in a particular manner even though it could not control or vary the field? The "poles" of its field are of course abstractions, but they are *there* and "pole" is a physically useful concept. In like manner does not the man who has isolated these positive traits of the human personality *observe* that his personality is aligned or polarized in a particular manner? To use the old-fashioned concept of action at a distance, does it not make sense for such man to say that the pole (God) acts upon his personality? As with the pole of the magnetic field, God (the pole) is an abstraction, but like the magnetic pole it is a useful part of the intellectual apparatus used to describe the phenomenon. I think therefore that it is meaningful for the man who has observed a polarity or focus of the human personality to say, "God is in me and I am in God." His abstraction is as indispensable to him as is the abstract magnetic pole to the physicist. It seems to me that the man who ignores the religious phenomenon is as culpable as the physicist would be who ignored the phenomenon of magnetism.

Dymon

What you're saying reminds me in some ways of Jung when he mentions "a supra-personal consciousness which is open to the sense of historical continuity." Jung finds this in the "collective unconscious". Remember too, that he very nearly allows a personification of this unconscious. He says:

"We might call it a collective human being combining the characteristics of both sexes, transcending youth and age, birth and death, and from having at his command a human experience of one or two million years, almost immortal." [42]

Eirat

I am not surprised that there may be parallels between what I have said and what Jung has said. What surprises me is that more people have not analyzed the matters we have discussed. I think, however, that there is this, among other differences between what I have said and what Jung said. Jung's "collective unconscious" may be similar to the "human personality" I have described. It matters not what you call it. But I say that man observes the abstract *object* of the positive traits I have described, and it is that which he calls God. He does not personify as God the human personality itself. The human personality is merely where he *finds* the abstraction. Would it not indeed be strange if man did *not* attempt to concretize this abstraction? Would he not be singularly unobservant if he did not *notice* it?

Dymon

If I have followed you correctly, you are then of opinion that a belief in God, at least as you have described it, is as well founded as a belief in anything else.

Eirat

Certainly it is. The only reason it hasn't appeared to be so to some theologians is because of their unrefined notions of what *science* is about on the one hand, and the lack of exactness in religion on the other.

Many theologians have never been able to reconcile science with religion as they understand it, and they either jettison their religion or hope devoutly that science will one day go away and leave them alone. A good many philosophers on the other hand appear to know little about either subject and have tended of late to restrict themselves to compiling syntactical dictionaries. This state of affairs is of course compounded by scientists who are so concerned with *measurable* phenomena that they are oblivious to all others.

[42] *Modern Man*, page 215.

75

EPILOGUE

Some persons who have read this book in draft form have asked, "What prompted you to write it?" I do not think that an answer to such question can throw light on the matters contained in the book. Indeed, the answer may be wholly irrelevant thereto. Such treatment as the book has attempted to make of its subject could have arisen from wholly different considerations than mine. Historically, however, my reasons, for whatever interest they may have, were as follows.

Mathematicians such as Peano and Frege, having early in this century discovered that much of mathematics could be derived from a few undefined postulates such as "number" and "successor of" were, as is well known, succeeded by Russell and Whitehead who showed that these postulates could in the main be derived from purely logical concepts such as "not", "all" and "some".[43] Thus, two subjects which historically had been considered unrelated, were joined. While there is some question as to the solidity of the joint, there can be no question that it has been made.

Much work has of course been done since that time purely in the specialist field of logic by Wittgenstein, Ramsey, Carnap and Stebbing (and of course by Russell himself), to name but a few. And that which has been done in logic has generally contributed to philosophy. Russell's theory of descriptions, first propounded early in this century, removed certain of the historical puzzles connected with the concept "existence". To quote an illustration used by Russell himself, it had been argued that if you say, "The golden mountain does not exist," you are saying that there is something that you are saying does not exist—namely, the golden mountain. Therefore the golden mountain must exist in some nebulous world, for otherwise the statement that it does not exist would have no meaning. But as Russell said, although the golden mountain may be grammatically the subject of a significant proposition, such a

[43] *Principia Mathematica.*

76

proposition when rightly analyzed no longer has such a subject. The proposition, "The golden mountain does not exist" becomes "the propositional function 'X is golden and a mountain' is false for all values of X." Here the phrase "does not exist" no longer occurs.

Similarly, Wittgenstein's early view, as set out in his "Tractatus", that a proposition is a picture of the facts which it asserts had a philosophical impact in its time (and still has).

He said that if you use the symbol "a R b" to represent the fact that "a" has the relation "R" to "b" (for example where "a" is to the left of "b", "R" represents "is to the left of"), your symbol is able to do so because it establishes a relation between "a" and "b" which *represents* the relation between "a" and "b". He said, "The gramophone record, the musical thought, the score, the waves of sound, all stand to one another in that pictorial internal relation, which holds between language and the world. To all of them the logical structure is common." [44]

He said further, "Propositions can *represent* the whole reality, but they cannot represent what they must have in common with reality in order to be able to represent it—the logical form. To be able to represent the logical form, we should have to put ourselves with the propositions outside logic, that is outside the world." [45]

At the end of World War I, the views of Wittgenstein and Russell parted company. Russell still thinks it possible that, although in any given language, there are things which that language cannot express, it is yet always possible to construct a language of higher order in which these things can be said.

It was implicit in Wittgenstein's view that (as he said), "Whereof one cannot speak, one must remain silent." It is implicit in Russell's view that there is nothing which cannot be said. Neither of them to my knowledge has modified these views. I agree with Wittgenstein's early view that a relation symbol is able to illustrate what it does because it *represents* the relation. I agree also that the comparison of the relation between, say, the record and the sound waves on the one hand, and language and the world on the other seems valid because one can envisage the gramophone needle picking up oscillations from the record and thereafter the speaker of the gramophone imposing the same structure on the sound waves. This is analogous to the human eye and the mind

[44] and [45] *Tractatus Logico Philosophicus.*

77

picking up relations in nature and the hand thereafter imposing the same structure in a painting. One might even accede to the view that the gramophone record *represents* the sound waves, as written language represents the world. Similarly, one can say that a painting represents the scene which is painted, but does this mean, as Wittgenstein suggested, that propositions cannot represent what the record has in common with the sound waves in order to be able to represent it? Can propositions not represent what a painting has in common with a scene in order to be able to represent it? Take a scene, a camera and a photograph instead of a painter (or indeed take a hologram taken by laser)—do the laws of optics not suffice to represent the relation between say, a scene and a photograph? Do the laws of propagation of sound not suffice to represent the relation between the phonograph record and the sound waves? It seems clear that these relations can be *described* in propositions. They can be described as well as any other observable physical relation. The relations of science are of course considerably more complex than pictorial symbols such as "to the left of", but at bottom are based upon such pictorial symbols.

Where then is the mystery, if mystery there still is? Is the relation between language and the world unique? Suppose for illustration a visitor from another galaxy—would he not describe this relation by reference to ostensive definitions, a descriptive dictionary compiled by himself, and the laws of grammar and syntax which he observed in use? Probably the relation between language and the world only *appears* unique because of the "I" of the observer (a concept I have discussed in this book). It appears unique in the same way that the relation between the gramophone record and the sound waves would appear unique to the gramophone if it had a mind. We are not, it seems to me, incapable of *representing* the relation between language and the world, unless of course we restrict "representation" to purely pictorial symbols. We simply describe and instruct in the use of language in lieu of representing the relation. If, as Wittgenstein stated, the relation were totally incapable of representation no one would ever learn to use language. It is therefore fruitless to ask what language has in common with nature so as to be able to represent it. It doesn't have *anything* in *common* with nature (any more than a label on a bottle has anything in common with the contents of the bottle).

The dilemma as first expressed by Wittgenstein does not for me exist. To him, however, it was of such power that he spent his remaining time (after writing the "Tractatus") investigating the use of language.[46] But he gave up the attempt to do so by means of logic. "The more narrowly we examine actual language, the sharper becomes the conflict between it and our requirement. (For the crystalline purity of logic was, of course, not a *result* of investigation; it was a requirement)." [47]

Not being able to accept Wittgenstein's original fiat that a proposition has something inexpressible in common with reality in order to be able to represent it, but being at the same time quite incapable of appreciating with Russell that the creation of the universe presents no logical difficulties,[48] I attempted for some time to explore the relation between the world and certain propositions about it. I found that these propositions (e.g. those about the "beginning of time" or those about "creation") were *not* able to represent the world. Further, it appeared that their failure in this respect did not arise from an absence of something inexpressible which they must have in common with reality. Indeed, that which they lack is quite expressible, as I hope I have been able in these pages to show. At the same time any attempt to express propositions of the kind I have mentioned in a language of higher order must be consigned to failure because the difficulty of such an attempt is certainly not one of finding sharper expressions.

[46] See the whole of his *Philosophical Investigations*.
[47] *Philosophical Investigations*, page 107.
[48] A view he reiterated in a letter to the author in May, 1965.

BIBLIOGRAPHY

Adler, I., *How Life Began,* 1957, New York, N.A. Library.
  Inside the Nucleus, 1963, New York, John Day.
Augustine, St., *Confessions,* Great Books, Encyclopedia Brit.
Ayer, A. J., *Language, Truth and Logic,* 2nd Ed., 1946, New
  York, Dover.
  The Foundations of Empirical Knowledge, 1963, Mac-
  millan.
Barnett, L., *The Universe and Dr. Einstein,* 1948, New York,
  Sloane.
Bergson, H., *Time and Free Will,* 1960, New York, Harper Bros.
Berkeley, G., *Principles of Human Knowledge, Three Dialogues
  Between Hylas and Philonous,* London, Smith, Peter.
  New Theory of Vision, New York, Everyman's Dutton.
Berrill, N. J., *You and The Universe,* 1958, New York, Dodd,
  Mead.
Blum, H. F., *Time's Arrow and Evolution,* 2nd Ed., 1962, New
  York, Harper Bros.
Bondi, H., *Cosmology,* 1960, Cambridge, Cambridge U.P.
Broad, C. D., *Five Types of Ethical Theory,* London, Humanities.
  Mind and Its Place in Nature, London, Humanities.
Carnap, R., *Logical Syntax of Language,* 1937, London,
  Humanities.
Conant, J. B., *On Understanding Science,* 1951, New Haven,
  Yale U.P.
De Broglie, L., *Physics and Microphysics,* 1960, New York, Har-
  per Bros.
Descartes, R., *Discourse on Method,* New York, Everyman's,
  Dutton.
DuNouy, L., *Human Destiny,* 1947, London, Longmans.
Dunn, L. C. and Dobzhansky, T., *Heredity, Race and Society,*
  1946, London, Longmans.

Eddington, A. S., *The Nature of the Physical World,* 1929, London, Macmillan.

    The Expanding Universe, 1932, Cambridge, Cambridge U.P.

    Space, Time and Gravitation, 1920, Cambridge, Cambridge U.P.

Einstein, A. and Infeld, L., *Evolution of Physics,* 1938, S and S.

Einstein, A., *Meaning of Relativity,* 1956, Princeton, Princeton U.P.

Fischer, L., *Gandhi, His Life and Work,* 1954, New York, N.A. Library.

Fraser, J. G., *The Golden Bough,* Macmillan.

Freud, S., *New Introductory Lectures on Psychoanalysis,* 1933, New York, Norton.

    Interpretation of Dreams, New York, Modern Library.

Gamow, G., *The Birth and Death of the Sun,* 1940, New York, Viking.

    One, Two, Three—Infinity, 1947, New York, N.A. Library.

    The Creation of the Universe, 1957, New York, Macmillan.

Haldane, J. B. S., *The Causes of Evolution,* 1932, London, Longmans.

Harrison, R. K., *The Dead Sea Scrolls,* 1961, New York, Harper Bros.

Hawkes, Jacquetta, *Prehistory.*

Horney, K., *New Ways in Psychoanalysis,* 1939, New York, Norton.

Hume, D., *Inquiry Concerning Human Understanding,* 1900, Chicago, Open Copyright.

Huxley, J., *Knowledge, Morality and Destiny,* 1957, New York, Harper Bros.

James, W., *Principles of Psychology,* New York, Dover.

    Varieties of Religious Experience, New York, Collier.

Jeans, J., *The Universe Around Us,* 4th Ed., 1945.

Jung, C. G., *Modern Man in Search of a Soul,* New York, Harcourt.

Kohler, W., *The Mentality of Apes,* London, Humanities.

Lovell, A. C., *The Individual and the Universe,* 1959, New York, Harper Bros.

McDougall, W., *Introduction to Social Psychology,* 1950, New York, Barnes & Noble.

Moore, G. E., *Principia Ethica*, 1903, Cambridge, Cambridge U.P.
    Philosophical Studies, 1959, Paterson, Littlefield, Adams.
Oparin, A. I., *The Origin of Life,* 1953, New York, Dover.
Poincare, H., *The Measure of Time,* 1913, London, Foundations of Science.
Prabhavananda, S. & Isherwood, C., *Bhagavad-Gita,* 1944, New York, Harper Bros.
Russell, B., *Inquiry into Meaning and Truth,* 1963, London, Pelican.
    Introduction to Mathematical Philosophy.
    My Philosophical Development, 1959, New York, Simon & Schuster.
    Mysticism and Logic, 1954, New York, Barnes & Noble.
    History of Western Philosophy, 1945, New York, Simon & Schuster.
    Nightmares of Eminent Persons, 1964, New York, Simon & Schuster.
Schweitzer, A., *The Quest of the Historical Jesus,* 1901, London, Macmillan.
Simpson, G., *The Meaning of Evolution,* 1951, New Haven, Yale U.P.
Spinoza, B., *Ethics,* New York, Everyman's, Dutton.
Stebbing, L. S., *Modern Introduction to Logic,* 5th Ed. 1949, New York, Barnes & Noble.
Sullivan, J. W., *The Limitations of Science,* 1933, New York, Viking.
    "The Physics and Chemistry of Life," 1955, New York, Scientific American.
Toynbee, A. J., *A Study of History,* 1946, Oxford, Oxford U.P.
Watson, I. B., *Behaviorism,* 1958, Chicago, U. of Chicago P.
White, M., *The Age of Analysis,* 1955, New York, Mentor.
Whitehead, A. N., *Science and The Modern World,* 1925, New York, Macmillan.
Whitehead, A. N. & Russell, B., *Principia Mathematica,* 1925-27, Cambridge, Cambridge U.P.
Wisdom, John, *Other Minds,* Philosophical Library.
Wittgenstein, L., *Tractatus Logico Philosophicus,* London, Humanities.
    Philosophical Investigations, 1958, London, Blackwell.